Better for Life

Better for Life

Turning Financial Hardship into Your Finest Hour

Daniel J. Jones

RESOURCE *Publications* · Eugene, Oregon

BETTER FOR LIFE
Turning Financial Hardship into Your Finest Hour

Resource Publications
An Imprint of Wipf and Stock Publishers
199 W. 8th Ave., Suite 3
Eugene, OR 97401
www.wipfandstock.com

ISBN 13: 978-1-60899-424-3

Manufactured in the U.S.A.

All persons in this book are real, and all stories in this book are true. However names and other information have been changed to protect the identities of those involved.

*For all those who continue to endure pain they never asked for:
God reserves the most exceptional trials for His most exceptional
subjects. Don't give up.*

To God be the glory.

"We are always on the anvil;
by trials God is shaping us for higher things."

—HENRY WARD BEECHER

Contents

Foreword

DANIEL JONES IS ONE of the bright young men that God is raising up to make an impact in his generation. I first came to know him as a student in my Homiletics class at Regent University (Virginia Beach) while he was working on his master's degree. He quickly established himself as one of the top students in my class because of his dedication to excellence and passion for the Lord.

His book entitled, *Better for Life* is a timely work that addresses the age-old philosophical question, "Why do bad things happen to good people?" Jones provides practical advice from a biblical perspective for people who are simply trying to get through another day because of the trials and tribulations they are facing as a result of life's circumstances, particularly the current global economic crisis.

Jones's work is encouraging because he is able to give hope to an audience that feels that they have been victimized by economic upheaval and rejection. *Better for Life* will help readers understand that despite their financial hardships, God is still in control, working everything together for their ultimate good. Of particular value is Jones's advice to believers to not be discouraged over getting *pink slips* from their jobs or rejection letters because it could mean that God is calling them to work for Him full-time in ministry.

Readers will benefit as they interact with the discussion questions after each chapter. They will also get great practical advice throughout the book, especially in Section Two, which gives simple methods on how to strengthen one's emotional and spiritual life and regain focus in order to become the person God has intended for them to become.

In essence, this book is not just another book on how to escape our trials and get back on the road to prosperity; rather, this volume seeks to make believers understand that the purpose that God has for our struggles is to make us *Better for Life*. I commend this book to all who want to seek a deeper understanding of the purpose that God has for them in the face of what appears to be impossible circumstances.

Charles R. Fox Jr., Ph.D.
Senior Pastor
Christ Community Church, Bowie, MD
Adjunct Professor, Regent University

Preface

Sometimes *you* choose what to do in life, and sometimes it is chosen *for* you. Writing this book is the latter. I would not have volunteered to write a book about going through hardships . . . until I encountered my own. At the time, my wife and I were dirt-poor and hosting a small group at seminary. As I prepared my weekly teaching, every Bible passage I encountered seemed to be about life's hardships. I just couldn't get away from it—so I taught it. Also, I began to notice how few mainstream books at that time (pre-recession 2007–2008) dealt with the subject. During prosperity booms, hardship books don't sell, I suppose. It frustrated me that so much Christian teaching was aimed at making "awesome people more *awesomer!*", instead of simply aiming to help broken and hurting people get through *just one more day*. So, with the encouragement of friends and family, I set-out to write what nobody else wanted to. But the greatest boost to my writing happened just before Christmas of 2008, when I lost my part-time minimum-wage job. With nothing left to lose, and tears streaming down my face, I spent my days and nights typing-out my small-group teachings. Now, after two years of living at an income of about half the poverty level, this book is finally complete.

For everyone who reads this book: I thank you for reading about *my* story, but it would be a shame if our partnership ended within these pages. You see, you have *your own* story, also. *Everyone* has a story to tell of their hardships, what they have learned through their trials and struggles, or even how this book has changed their life for the better. Moreover, as a writer, I know what it is like to have so very much to say, but no forum to communicate it. Well, *now is your opportunity*. I invite *you* to *tell your story* on this book's website: www.BetterForLifeBook.com. You see, *your* story is just as important as mine, and it is probably even more powerful. And as much as you would like the opportunity to *tell* your story, there are hundreds of other struggling people who *need to hear* your story. Be an instrument of hope to encourage and inspire others to get through their own hardships by sharing your story on this website, and directing others to it.

For those who are *not* struggling financially: I hope that you consider reading this book as a means to become aware of the myriad of reasons why so many around you *are* struggling financially. Real wisdom is to learn from another's experiences. Who knows . . . if you will learn the lessons of this book *now*, then you just might save yourself from much difficulty *later*.

At the end of each chapter are "Discussion Questions," intended to be used in church small groups, or support-group settings. I pray that *Better for Life* may be an acceptable resource to encourage financially-struggling individuals and families in these intimate settings. For church pastors: please feel welcome to teach whatever you find herein that would benefit the struggling members of your congregations. After all, it is not *my* material—it is the Lord's.

I never intended to write a great book about God, and I hope you don't consider this as such. Instead, my goal has always been to write a book about a *great* God. I did not write *Better for Life* for scholars to applaud or the renowned to admire; I expect none of those things. Instead, I wrote it to give *an ounce of hope* to broken and hurting people who have none, just as *I* had none. If it accomplishes this, then I will thank my Lord for the tremendous honor and privilege. So, as much as I hope you enjoy *Better for Life*, above all, I pray that it will help you get through *just one more day*.

Acknowledgments

Without a *very* special wife, this book would never have been written. Thank you, Soiky, for your love and support—I will always cherish you. Thanks to Jonathan and Ariel for understanding that, "daddy has to write his book." And now we'll finally have time to play together! I appreciate the support of my mom and dad, Kelli, K-fur, Russ, Cliff, Kerri, Elizabeth, Kimi-toes, Ellie & Jim, Chris, and Groovy (from whom I got my sense of humor), Rhonda, along with my cousins and in-laws, and *all* the spouses. We love you all, and are proud to call you *family*. We are thankful for the precious families who have been the instruments of God's love in our lives: the West, the Burchetts, the Fernandeses, the Arbours, the Flamms, the Morillos, the Andersons, the Aranas, the Kangs, the Ims, the Marianos, our other church friends and Regent pals, Vivian, Brenton, Meghan, and our friends at Malta. Good friends can stick closer than family, and we count you as both. Many thanks to the R.U. Library and Cafeteria for providing work and friendship when we needed both. Thanks to the Young Kwang Presbyterian Church for believing in me. Dr. Fox, Rabbi Rosenfarb, Pastor Martel, Pastor Hwang, Dr. Newberg, Pastor John, Dr. Rieke, and Pastor Randolph: thank you for your leadership and teaching, but most of all, for your kindness. We are grateful to the Azalea Church food pantry, the King's Pantry, and the VB WIC programs for feeding us when we were hungry. Our sincere thanks to Glen Ryder—the best realtor in Virginia Beach, as far as I'm concerned. And last, much thanks to the Wipf and Stock Publishing team for taking a chance on me.

1

Foundations

Storms Don't Discriminate

(MATTHEW 7:24–27)

Religion converts despair, which destroys, into resignation,
which submits.

—MARGUERITE GARDINER, COUNTESS OF BLESSINGTON

STORMS AT SEA CAN be frightening. As a cadet onboard my first merchant marine ship, I leaned over the rail of the 800-foot vessel, hypnotized by the trail of churning water as San Francisco faded away. And I *hoped* for a storm.

In the years prior, I listened to incredible "sea stories" from experienced sailors who faced the ocean's fury with nothing but bare hands and a sailor's intuition, and lived to tell the tale. I was captivated by those intense stories of triumph, and would visualize every detail in my mind. Finally aboard a merchant vessel, I was hoping to earn my own exploits which I could share with wide-eyed listeners around an evening fire. Within two weeks of leaving San Francisco I got my wish. A tropical cyclone stood between us and our next port, Japan.

On merchant ships, the captain knows the limits of his or her vessel. Safety is obviously the number one concern in the industry, but expediency is number two. Assuming the safety of the vessel, cargo, and personnel, the captain takes the route which will get his ship to the next port the fastest. In the transportation industry, time is not only money, it is *big* money. On routes of expediency, sometimes storms are simply unavoidable. And they can punish a ship for days.

The ship might find herself heading directly into the storm, gliding up one wave and crashing violently down the next. If you were to stand at one end of a large merchant vessel during heavy seas, you would actually see the hull *bend* with each rise and slam of the bow. Further, the eerie metallic groans would send chills up your spine as you realize the only thing keeping you alive in an angry ocean is flexing, bending steel. Only then do you recognize your vulnerability, and grasp the fact *there is no escape.*

Today there is another storm blanketing America, and the rest of the world. This colossal storm threatens the livelihood of billions of people. It is an economic storm. *Nobody is safe; everybody is vulnerable.*

America has lost a staggering number of jobs in 2009 and 2010. People's incomes and savings have been slashed, and there is no guarantee of how much more will be lost. Please don't make the mistake of thinking this is restricted to the poor. Even the wealthiest people in America have been severely affected. In fact, not even one American has been completely insulated from it. Every single person has been adversely affected by today's worldwide financial problems. Through it all, everybody wants to know how to make the pain go away. The overarching question in everybody's minds is: "With the economy getting worse by the day, is there anything I can do to keep myself safe?"

To most people, unemployment data is nothing more than numbers— digits in a row. However, each statistical unit represents a *real person*, often an entire family, who depended on their lost income to make it through the next month. They have housing expenses to pay. But this month it won't get paid. They have credit cards and car payments, electricity and telephone bills, which also won't be funded this month. And not only are there millions of jobs which have been lost in America, but there are now millions more people competing for the ones that remain. So the chances of simply finding another job have also dramatically decreased.

You have probably noticed how millions of lost jobs have affected you and those around you. Maybe you lost *yours*. At the very least, you know somebody who has recently lost theirs. More people are cutting personal expenses any way they can. I know of a barber shop which grossed a mere $39 (including tips) one day recently. And it's not just small shops which are affected, either. Last week a Wal-Mart employee told me that if their sales do not soon rebound, the management will make "real cutbacks" in the form of lay-offs. When even Wal-Mart struggles, you *know* times are tough.

Maybe your situation was different than a job-loss. You might be one of the retired or nearly-retired workers who lost up to 75% of your retirement savings. Now you'll have to work for another decade just to afford to retire. Or, maybe you are qualified for upper-level positions, but since the employment market is saturated with talent and experience, you can only obtain lower-level (and lower-paying) positions. Possibly you are one of the lucky ones who have kept your job, thankful for a mere decrease in pay, as you watch others pushed out the door. Yet you are still not insulated from the tough times, as each day you wonder if you will be the next to go.

The unnerving thing is this economic turmoil *has no etiquette.* No polite courtesy. It simply ravages everything - and everybody - that comes in its path. Jobs: terminated. Businesses: snuffed out. 401 (k)'s: devastated. Retirement plans: wiped out. Families: shattered. Individuals: suicide.

Clearly, today's financial upheaval does not discriminate. It disregards gender, class, and income, but simply wreaks havoc on *everybody*. It does not care who you are or what you've done in life. Nor does it care that you were about to retire, or that you have a family to feed. It is a storm raging out of control which devastates all it reaches. And it has reached the entire world.

This storm is affecting the lives of those who had been unwise in their financial dealings, as well as those who had been extremely wise in their monetary decisions. Case in point, as of early 2009, Bill Gates lost $18 billion, and Warren Buffet lost $25 billion.[1] From the poorest of the poor to the richest of the rich, all have been negatively affected. My point is this: *it's not your fault.* This is very difficult for many of us to accept, because since birth we have been groomed to take responsibility for everything which happens in life.

We live in a "blame or be blamed" culture. When something goes wrong, finger-pointing is the first thing to follow. You either blame someone else (or yourself), or you get blamed by them. There is no third option when something goes wrong. When the dog makes a mess on the carpet, we accept the blame, because it wouldn't have happened if we had trained him better. When the car breaks down, we take responsibility, because it probably made a weird noise and we did not check it immediately. Culture has mandated that when *anything* goes wrong, *there must be a responsible party.* No longer are there simple no-fault accidents.

To top it off, whenever something bad happens and we do not immediately accept the blame, others are quick to bestow it upon us. When we arrive late to work, never mind that our commute was extended by forty-five minutes because of an accident; the boss tells us we should plan our commute expecting such "unexpected circumstances." When our teenager does something they shouldn't, the in-laws are quick to point out that it never would have happened if we were more responsible parents.

Somehow we are placed in a role of being a demigod in control of every minute aspect of every element of life, including dog's accidents, children's choices, automobile malfunctions, and anything else with a negative consequence. Everything in life is somehow accounted to be under our control. This is neither right, nor healthy.

The simple truth is, sometimes the dog's bladder just can't expand any further, so they make an accident on the carpet. Children really do have their own functioning brain which empowers them to make independent choices. Sometimes metallic objects break before anybody expected them to. And sometimes an economy tanks when people thought it was strong.

What I'm saying is that Titanic-events still happen, and today's economic collapse is one of them. America seemed to be doing so well over the past few years. Business was booming, real estate was roaring, and stocks were soaring. It's not your fault that you didn't see around the blind corner of America's economic destiny. Few people did.

Moreover, even if you had known in advance, it would have done you little good. Sure, you could have saved a little more, but you still would have lost your job. You could have made adjustments to your nest-egg, but your company's retirement account still would have gone belly-up, and forced you back into the workforce. And at the end of the day, you still would have had more month than money. Few of us saw a financial crash coming, but *none* of us had anything we could do about it.

The point is, it's time to stop blaming ourselves for our financial problems, and start figuring out *what to do about them.* What's done is done, and now each of us has a choice to make. Will you allow your natural "fight or flight" instincts to take-over, or will you use your circumstances as an opportunity to become a *better you*? You can fight the system all you want by pointing fingers and issuing blame, but it won't restore your lost money. You can run away, hide under your bed, and cry until things get better. But this will not resolve your problems, either. *Or* you can allow God to make you a stronger and better person through your misfortunes, and become *better for life.*

You see, just because it's not your fault doesn't mean God can't use it to make you into a better *you* . . . He can and *He will,* if you let Him. God is in the people business, and specifically, the business of making people better. His specialty is taking broken-down lives and restoring them to be beautiful and strong. God could have intervened to stop this storm before it devastated your life, but then you never would have had this opportunity to grow as a person. Neither would I. I am not implying that this storm is desirable, but I am saying that you can benefit from it *if* you respond appropriately. If you are willing, today's messy situation can be the springboard you have been waiting for in life. This problem can be your greatest turning point!

On merchant ships, the experienced captain trusts the integrity of his ship to weather a storm. He knows exactly what his ship was designed and built to withstand, so he fears little in the way of storms. The rest of the crew may wonder if they will ever see their families again, but the captain knows better. The ship will make it through the storm. And in my first "sea story," that is just where we went—*through* the storm. More specifically, we went through the eye of the tropical cyclone. We secured everything not already tied-down, and were taken for the *ride of our lives.*

For three days the ship was locked into a disconcerting cycle. The bow would quickly rise upward, and then slam violently downward with a force which shook the entire ship. The vessel rolled a total of seventy degrees, from side to side. Anything not tied down was thrown to the floor ("deck" in nautical terms), and stayed there for the duration of the storm. One refrigerator broke away from its wall-mounting and slammed from wall to wall for a full day; nobody was foolish enough to try to stop a major appliance on the loose. Career sailors stayed pinned in their beds (or "racks"), dressed in their bright-orange lifesaving immersion suits for days. In their minds, the question was not *if* we would sink, but *when* we would sink. And even though our twenty-two-knot steamship was at full speed ahead, the storm pushed against us at twenty-*five* knots; our speed-over-ground was three knots *backwards.*

That tropical cyclone was by far the most frightening thing I had experienced in all my nineteen years of life. During it, I was convinced I would never have the opportunity to tell my *only* sea story. Others on-board also thought life would end before reaching Japan. But through it all, the captain knew we would make it. He had been sailing for nearly fifty years, with over a dozen as master of that particular vessel. He knew every inch of his steamship, and he knew it could handle every ounce of that storm. *And it did.*

God knows *you* even better than that salty sea captain knew his ship. And He knows that you are able to weather your storm, too. Going through physical or fiscal storms can be scary business, but the Captain of your life knows your limits, and He will safely guide you through this and *all* of your personal storms, and even use them for *your advantage.* He will do this because *God is interested in your growth, not your comfort.* So, He is not averse to using a storm to make *you* a better you.

Today's economic hurricane is huge, and it affects everyone to some degree. Some of us are stuck in the very epicenter of fury, while others are on the edge of the storm and only feel reduced effects. Yet each of us has some portion of the storm affecting us. It is not fun for anybody, and we all wish it would *just stop.* We want somebody to hold-back the gale of economic turmoil, so we can rest. If someone could put an end to the crashing waves of hardship, and halt the tsunami-like floods of debt, then we could get back to enjoying life once again. We just wish somebody could *stop the storm*, and the pain it brings. But they can't. There is no quick antidote, or easy solution. This is not a storm which we can go around. The only way to pass this storm is to go *through* it.

Jesus talked about the storms of life, just like the economic one we are facing today. However, contrary to the teachings of some, Jesus did not give a quick-fix solution. He did not offer a "get out of storms free" card, neither did He provide a "give and get rich" guarantee. I'll grant that it works sometimes . . . but not always. Case in point: Jesus did not guarantee financial abundance to the widow who gave her very last two coins to God's work, so it just doesn't compute how someone today could make promises beyond those made by Christ Himself. In addition, the original Apostles were known for many great things, but wealth was not one of them. If riches were the ultimate fruit of godliness, then those Apostles were rotten to the core.

Some of these *get-rich-with-God* teachings originate from corrupt individuals shamelessly selling salvation (or other blessings) for a price. Others are sincere enough to *want* everybody to receive financial abundance without being mature enough to *appreciate* that the divine plan differs from person to person. The truth is that not all Christians are meant to be financially endowed. Certainly some are. However, the duties of most in God's Kingdom lie in other areas, like teaching, exhorting, or showing mercy (for others, see Romans 12:6–8). Since Jesus was all-wise, He understood that the master plan differed from person to person. And since He wasn't selling anything (salvation, in the least), He didn't use the *get out of storms free* gimmick to fill the coffers.

Jesus explained that the storms of life happen to everybody, including His followers. Nobody is exempt from the effects of sin in this world. Further, we are not able to stop most of our storms, and very rarely can we go around them. So, Jesus taught a different approach to handling the storms of life. He taught how to *out-last* them.

You see, by definition, storms must fizzle out. In nature, they must wear-out themselves so completely that they are exhausted of every last ounce of intrinsic energy. Only then will things return to "normal." This economic storm is no different. It also must die-out . . . eventually. If you and I can just hold-on for a little while longer, then we will be alright. And Jesus gave us the secret to holding-out for the long-haul, to outlast the storms of life. At the end of His longest recorded teaching, based mostly upon individual lifestyle and ethics, Jesus unabashedly declares:

> Therefore, whoever hears these sayings of Mine, and does them, I will liken him to a wise man who built his house on a rock: and the rain descended, the floods came, and the winds blew and beat on that house; and it did not fall, for it was founded on the rock. But everyone that hears these sayings of Mine, and does not do them, will be like a foolish man who built his house on the sand: and the rain descended, the floods came, and the winds blew and beat on that house; and it fell. And great was its fall (Matthew 7:24–27, NKJV).

You see, you may not have realized it, but you are a builder. So am I. Actually, everybody is. We are each building our own "house," which is Jesus' picturesque way of describing our lives. Your house/life is a culmination of all of the choices you have made, and continue to make, each one based upon the information which you have come in contact with. Let me explain.

When somebody wants to build a house, a suitable piece of ground is first chosen, and then a concrete foundation is laid on that ground. The idea is to provide a solid and immobile anchor for the upcoming structure to attach to. Next the wood framing is added, followed by brickwork, drywall, windows, etc.

Likewise, each one of us is presented with information, or truth-claims. The information is the ground. Of necessity, we make personal assessments of that information. Our assessment is the foundation which we lay upon that ground. And the subsequent actions are the upward structure which we built upon that foundation. Every one of our actions is in some way based upon our own personal worldview. What kind of car you choose to drive is not only dictated by your family size and needs, but also depends on your views of nature and mankind's responsibility to care for it. Your dietary and exercise habits are determined by your level of concern for your health.

In the same way, each of our decisions and actions is a brick or a wooden 2-by-4 which we build upon our foundation of belief. For example, how kind we are to others is a reflection of the inherent value which we place upon others, which is based upon our assessment of God's word. Jesus instructs each of us to be kind even to our enemies (Luke 6:35–36). If we believe that Jesus speaks the truth, then we will practice being kind to all people and thereby build our house on this foundational truth. If we act cruelly or indifferently toward others, then our actions are proof that we do not assess Jesus' word to be truth. In this case, we build our house upon *our own* estimation of mankind's value. So, regardless of our worldviews, we are each building our *house*. With each action or inaction, the structure is rising, whether we realize it or not. As we build upward, each of our houses might appear to be grand and beautiful. But the upward structure won't keep the house anchored in a storm. Only the *foundation* can accomplish that.

This is where Jesus comes in. He makes a truth-claim: "Do what I say and you will be building your life on solid rock. Ignore what I say and you will be building your life on shifting sand. But either way remember, the storm is coming" (Matthew 7:24–27, paraphrased). For years we have each been building our lives upon our personal assessment of Jesus' truth-claim. But now the storm is here, and our foundations are being tested. The winds, rains, and floods are pounding against our lives, and only a rock-solid foundation will keep a person's house (and life) standing strong. A weak foundation of sand will inevitably cause the downfall of the beautiful house upon it. Make no mistake, today foundations are being tested and their substance is being revealed. People's very lives hang in the balance.

Just watch the news and you'll see what I'm talking about. A wealthy banker commits suicide because he lost a couple zeros in his personal financial portfolio: sand. A family of six loses everything they own, but they still go to church and trust God to provide food today: rock. A marriage ends in bitter divorce from the loveless battles waged over money: sand. A single mother works two part-time jobs to keep her family afloat: solid rock. It's easy to recognize people's foundations, if you know what to look for. The things which last are built upon something more substantial than elastic green paper; they are built upon Jesus Christ.

There is little doubt that each day life is getting more difficult for many in America. The bar of life's circumstances is set high above our abilities. Many of us Christians hope and even expect God to valiantly gallop into our situation and *save the day*. We want God to *rescue us* from our bills while still allowing us to maintain the lifestyle to which we have grown accustomed in affluent America. In other words, we are praying for an unexpected six-digit check to arrive in the mail, or the grace to win the Lotto.

We want God to simply fix out problems, and thereby lower the bar of life's circumstances . . . but I don't believe He will. I think God has a better way for us to overcome the difficult circumstances every one of us faces. Instead of "rescuing" us by lowering the bar (so we can sluggishly crawl over it), God wants to help us become stronger, so we can rise to the level of our circumstances and overcome them. Instead of lowering the standard to accommodate our weakness and lethargy, God intends to increase our ability so we can vault over the full height of the bar. In other words, *God isn't concerned with making life better for you; He is interested in making* you *better for life.*

Many of us have been taught that success is found in an employment position, and happiness is proportional to our paycheck. However, even a quick glance at the supermarket tabloids will prove that neither fame nor fortune brings lasting happiness. Hollywood's rich and famous include some of the most miserable people I have ever seen! Further, if success can be gained in the bestowal of a position, then it can be eliminated at the loss of one. In contrast, the truth is that *real* success and *true* happiness are closely connected, and both last longer than a paycheck or a position. True success and happiness cannot be separated from the more important things in life, like faithfulness, compassion, and character. These things out-last a job—they last a lifetime.

I am convinced that if Jesus were living in a human body on planet earth today, He would not be the U.S. president or a Fortune-500 company CEO. He was on no quest for power or money 2000 years ago, so there is no reason to think He would seek these things today. Further, as the deeded Inheritor of the world, He didn't have to stab anybody in the back to gain it. Instead, Jesus did the opposite: He *laid down His own life* so others could share His inheritance with Him.

If Jesus were walking the earth again today, He'd probably be a manual laborer, just like He was back then. Maybe He would do the carpentry thing again, or maybe He'd fix cars this time. But one thing's for sure: Jesus certainly wouldn't hold a tax-refund telethon to keep His ministry on the air. Without a doubt Jesus was different. Nothing to gain. Nothing to prove. Nothing fancy. Just Jesus. Maybe today we've lost focus of what's really important. And just maybe this economic crisis is God's way of prodding the American church to refocus on those main priorities once again.

Those who have trusted in money have sadly built their lives upon the sand. Lives built upon sand will crumble. They *must* crumble. Nevertheless, those who trust in the everlasting God will remain steadfast because they have built upon solid rock. When the tempest hits, either the person outlasts the storm, or the storm destroys the person. The foundation alone makes the difference. And those lives built upon the rock of Jesus Christ will *always* survive their storms.

The first step to becoming *better for life* is to put your trust in Jesus. Only a life built upon the rock of Jesus Christ will outlast the storms of life. Is it too late to build upon this rock? Not if you're still breathing. You *will* face the storm regardless. Your experience might be only the soft outer winds, or you might receive the full brunt of the storm's epicenter passing over your life. You may lose your career, your friends, your house, and who knows what else. Those things you cannot control. But you *can* control what (or Who) you anchor to, and if you anchor to Jesus, you'll make it through. You'll have enough stability and hope to outlast the dark nights of your life. To take this step only takes a simple decision to count Jesus' words as truth, and begin living-out those words. You really don't have anything to lose, but everything to gain, not the least of which is stability and hope. And let's face it; you'll need *both* to make it through this storm.

Nevertheless, Jesus offers something more than basic stability and hope to get by. Merely getting by is not the goal. *Success* is the goal. *Absolute victory* is the aim. God's objective is to shape you and strengthen you to stare in the face of what you have most feared (financial instability, future uncertainties, a painful existence, even death) and not even bat an eye. When your greatest fears materialize, God will help you to brazenly and courageously overcome them all. To "make lemonade out of lemons" is to put it too lightly. This is more like grabbing a hungry lion by the mane and taking a bite out of *him*. And once you do, you won't fear lions anymore. Jesus has already been there; He has gone before us. The world gave Jesus its *best shot*, but He still got up and overcame the world (John 16:33). Death tried to finish-off Jesus, but He turned right around and abolished death in return! (1 Timothy 1:10). This is why He alone is able to teach you and lead you to overcome through *your* situation.

This purest form of success and victory is irrespective of the appearance of the outcome. Appearances can be very deceiving. 2000 years ago the Jewish religious leaders thought they had eternally silenced Jesus' voice and message by arranging for His crucifixion. By all outward appearances they had succeeded; they had finished-off the "King of the Jews." Even Jesus' closest friends and disciples wept at the loss of His tremendous life. Nobody had any suspicion that there was a *part B* to Jesus' life. And certainly nobody had any clue that the "sequel" would be more glorious than the original. If we follow Jesus' leading, then this will be our story, too. Jesus' successful navigation of His difficult crucifixion event was the single greatest factor which propelled Him into glory.

After Jesus' crucifixion, a pair of His disciples were lamenting over their crushed hope of being delivered by their Messiah. In the midst of their discussion, Jesus Himself entered the conversation and answered, "Oh foolish ones, and slow of heart to believe all that the prophets have spoken! Ought not the Christ to have suffered these things and to enter into his glory?" (Luke 24:25–26, NKJV). Jesus *had* to suffer before entering His glory. One common law in God's economy is that *suffering is always followed by glory*, and conversely, *glory is always preceded by suffering*.

The idea is, before God ever breaks-down something, He already has the intention and the plan to rebuild it even stronger. This is what happened with Jesus, and this is what is happening with *you*. It is the reason why so many of us are going through trying seasons of life. Growth seasons stretch us and pull us like no other times in life. We feel like our lives are in shambles, and broken pieces. Our emotions are exhausted, and it takes all of our willpower to hold back the tears as we try to get through another difficult day. It seems as though life is against us, and there is nobody who can help.

You probably feel like you are going through this all alone also; just like David standing alone before the giant Goliath. However, David had significant past experience which made him the only person in Israel who was able to defeat the giant who stood before him. Through his years of shepherding God had prepared David for *that specific fight*. And don't think even for an instant that God has done any less with you. *God has prepared you for just this moment—your* moment. You can rest assured that you are prepared for the challenge. Just like David, you are well-able to overcome the giant problems standing before you!

I'll grant that you might have helped get yourself into your mess; many of us did by making uninformed financial decisions. However, the worldwide economic collapse played the *major* role in forming your problems, and this was not your fault. Further, the mere fact that you are reading this book tells God that you are serious about letting Him change your life for the better, and *He will honor this decision*.

Even though it may seem that major components of your life remain unsecured, and are slamming back and forth with threatening force, remember: *God is not mad at you*. Although you may feel like everything is falling to pieces around you, and you are barely holding life together, remember: *everything will be ok*. And even though you are doing the best you can to go forward in life, but find that your storm is still pushing you backwards, *don't give-up*. God has a plan for you. You will see that plan to completion, if you will only trust Him.

It is easy to become discouraged and depressed if we feel like we are subject to endless challenges without purpose. However, if we know the *reason* for those challenges, we can stand tall and strong through them all. In the following chapters we will investigate several Biblical characters to uncover insights into the specific reasons for their struggles, and learn how they ultimately overcame. You will understand the purposes which God has for you in *your* trials. As you see God's methods and purposes played out in the lives of these Bible characters, you will grow confident and able to stand strong in your troubles, trusting that God has a purpose for *your* trial and your *life*. In short, instead of being overcome by your trials, you will overcome *them*.

Through Section One of this book (chapters 2–7), you will discover several different key purposes which might specifically apply to you in your situation today. You could be in the middle of the hardest test of your life because of your commitment to God. Or, maybe God is using you as an agent of grace in your storm to open up the hearts of those near you. God may be using this economic tsunami to transition you into your place of promise-fulfillment. Through your financial disaster, you might find that God is calling you into Christian service. Possibly your discomfort is God's instrument to expand your ministry effectiveness. Or, God might have a greater heavenly reward awaiting you for your dedication and obedience through this storm. This section by no means exhausts every possible scenario, but is intended to give understanding and hope to those of us who may have lost both.

As you continue reading chapters 8–14 (Section Two) of this book, you will discover how to improve your life while you are in your storm. Remember, God is not so concerned with making life better for you; He is interested in making you *better for life*. In this section you will discover the major lessons I learned through my own economic hardships. In addition, you will be given several practical methods to *spiritually strengthen yourself*.

I do not claim that these techniques will put an end to your economic storm. In fact, the truth is they are not intended to change your circumstances in the least. These practices are meant to fortify you today, so you can *outlast* and *overcome* your storm. They will not lower the bar of your trials, but they will strengthen you to leap over that bar. When life gets tough don't get discouraged, and don't give-up . . . just get tougher. Light always shines brightest in the darkness. And if life seems pretty dark for you right now, then *now* is your time to grow and shine. Make the most of it! Use your hardships as God intended: become *better for life*!

Discussion Questions:

1   How has today's economic storm affected you personally? How has it affected others you know? How does this make you feel?

2   Are the affects of today's difficult economy restricted to class, income, or good/bad financial decisions? Explain.

3   Is God more concerned about your personal comfort or your personal growth in life? Which one are *you* most concerned about?

4   What did Jesus teach about getting through the storms of life?

5   What does it take to "build a house" upon a rock, and how does one begin doing this?

6   What is God's idea of "success," and how does this compare to the world's definition of success? Do you need to reevaluate your idea of what it means to be successful?

7   How does God intend to get you over the bar of life's circumstances?

8   What does God do with broken-down lives? How could this apply to you personally?

9   Can a Christian truly determine their spirituality by observing their outward circumstances? Why or why not?

10   What should be the goal for a Christian who is facing hardship?

SECTION ONE

God, Why Is This Happening To Me?

2

But I Did Everything Right!

Job: Only the Best Take the Test

(JOB 1–2, 23, 42)

*A gem cannot be polished without friction,
nor a man perfected without trials.*

—CHINESE PROVERB

REMEMBER SCHOOL? WE ALL have memories of classes and text books and homework. Hopefully you were a gifted student who did well in all your courses with little effort. Or maybe you had to fight to get your mediocre grades. You might have struggled before major tests, as you studied all night to prepare, like I did. After all, you couldn't afford to "bomb" a major examination worth 50% of your course grade!

Don't forget about the pop-quizzes sprung on you by your math teacher! Math instructors are famous for giving pop-quizzes. You might still get sweaty-palmed when you recall taking them. I sure do. As un-prepared as you felt, you were compelled to demonstrate your grasp of the material, or go down in a blaze of glory trying. The only redeeming factor was that pop-quizzes were worth only a small percentage of your overall grade, so even if you failed one from time to time, you could still earn a decent grade.

But how would you have felt if your math instructor gave you a *pop final-exam*? You might have struggled through the test, possibly leaving entire sections blank, all because *you were not ready*. You might have been perturbed at the situation, or even outraged at the injustice!

After all, you were not given proper advanced notice. *Nobody told you to prepare for it!* Job knew the feeling well, because this is exactly what happened to him. God sprung upon Job the greatest faith-test of his entire life, and *didn't even mention it was a test.*

From time to time God puts every Christian through pop-faith-tests, and rarely informs any of us about these examinations. For example, life was going swimmingly, and out of the blue you got a pink slip on your desk: your position has been terminated. Your marriage relationship seemed above-average, until you arrived home and discovered an empty house and a scribbled note: your spouse wants out. After decades of eating right and exercising, you found a lump: cancer has begun.

Tests from God can come in the form of job losses, struggles at work, financial difficulties, marital problems, health issues, or even trouble with children. And *none of us* are immune from these tests. Sure, we might get one particular area in good working order (say, our finances), but there is no guarantee that health problems aren't just around the corner. Regardless of the specific area of our testing, *every* believer gets tested in their lifetime.

Most of us would not take issue with God over these faith-tests, if only we knew it was a test. But the problem is God doesn't offer us warning by giving us His examination schedule. More often than not, He simply springs these *pop*-faith-tests on us, as with Job. As we watch our lives falling to pieces before our eyes we don't even know how to react.

This is often compounded by the fact that during these tests, God rarely gives us direction. In fact, God can seem altogether distant. There is no relief in Bible-reading. A short 10-minute devotional used to be enough to keep you joyful throughout your day, but now you search the Scriptures for hours and still can't find peace. Even prayer doesn't seem to "work" for you anymore. You spend hours on your knees hoping for *hope*, but none comes. You plead, "If I did something wrong just let me know and I'll repent, I'll change, I'll make amends—God, please just show me how to get out of this mess?" But no answer comes.

It seems doubly cruel of God to subject His children to torturous trials, and then give us the silent treatment. Whereas we used to enjoy walking in His light and fellowship, now it seems like we are walking in darkness alone. How do you know when you are being given a pop-faith-test? When everything which *can* go wrong *has* gone wrong, but

God still has not told you that you are at fault—you are being tested. Of course God does not spoon-feed us the answers to our difficulties at these times. No professor gives the answers while the test is in progress. And, like many examinations, it is to be done alone. So we experience loneliness.

Sometimes this feeling can be so intense it seems like you are drowning in loneliness. The thought of having to walk out the front door to face the world is a dreadful one. So you try to suppress this deep-seated feeling to get through your day in a somewhat sociable manner, but it doesn't work very well. The clock never seemed quite so slow before. Every second you are forced to be around others feels like an eternity, as you struggle to maintain some measure of composure. You wish you could have a heart-to-heart talk with *somebody* who can relate to what you're going through. Yet nobody *can* relate. You might be alright if you could just hide from the world. But you can't. Life won't stop and wait for you to get through this. It just keeps going. Have you ever been there?

All this is wrapped-up in your difficulties. It is these problems which thrust you into despair. "If my problems would go away, then everything would return to normal and life would be fine," you reason. But the problems don't stop. Instead, they keep piling up higher and higher. Each day more bills arrive, and more debt collectors call. The only reason these callers abstain during the night hours is because the law prohibits it (I learned this from experience). Rent is due, the telephone and electricity are about to be cut-off, the car is out of gas, and your bank account is in the single-digits. To top it off, there is no help in sight. You probably didn't even have the money to buy this book—somebody else *gave* it to you!

I'm not just talking about having a rough week; I'm talking about having a rough *life*. Depression soon sets in. You retreat to bed often, just so you can release your sobs. By the time your feet touch the floor in the morning you have already passed the best part of your day—it can only go downhill from there. This is a dark, lonely, and scary place to be in life. The only thing you want is *a way out*. Maybe you are there right now. I've been there, and so has Job. In fact, Job has probably experienced this more deeply than anybody. You might have heard about his story or read it in the Bible. As we take a look at Job's pop-faith-test, you just might discover that you have a lot more in common with Job than you thought.

Job was wealthy and well respected in his day. He was a prominent social leader, a loving husband, a doting father, and a businessman par-excellence. Job was both righteous and religious. He not only showed-up for religious services on a regular basis, but he lived-out his faith every day of the week. He was the epitome of godliness. God Himself described Job saying, "... *there is* none like him in the earth, a blameless and upright man, one who fears God and shuns evil" (Job 1:8b, NKJV), and everybody for miles around knew it.

Job was blessed with seven sons and three daughters (Job 1:2). He was not only a father, but a terrific one who did a wonderful job raising his children. All of them were well-adjusted individuals who maintained their family ties (Job 1:4). Job was also an exceptional business owner, using his wisdom and diligence to amass great wealth. He was a mas-ter investor who diversified his holdings to ensure the longevity of his portfolio. Job was held in the highest esteem by people near and far, who knew Job to be "the greatest of all the people of the East" (Job 1:3b, NKJV). He might have even held the title of "Mr. Ancient Near-East"!

However, Job's story turns tragic when messengers report several freak accidents nearly simultaneously. "A neighboring tribe came and stole all of your oxen and donkeys, and killed all of the workers but me," one said (Job 1:14–15, paraphrased). Right then another interrupted, "Fire fell from heaven and burnt-up all of your sheep and servants ex-cept me" (Job 1:16, paraphrased). Before this messenger could finish his report, another arrived and blurted-out, "Another tribe attacked us and stole all of your camels and killed all of the workers but me" (Job 1:17, paraphrased). But the worst news came from the fourth messenger, "a tornado destroyed your son's house while all ten of your children were eating there, and now they are all dead" (Job 1:18–19, paraphrased).

Words cannot describe how badly Job was devastated. He lost all of his oxen and donkeys, which were used to farm his lands, so he could no longer farm. He lost all of his camels, leaving him nothing to trade with. He lost all of his wool-making sheep ... and by *fire from heaven*, of all things! When you lose your livelihood by fire coming from the sky, you've got *real problems*. All but four of his manual laborers (who ran the entire aggregate business) died. To top it off, Job lost all ten of his beloved children. The only thing he had left was a nagging spouse. Life could hardly get worse.

The man who was once the envy of the East became the shame of society within a few short minutes. Getting this far into this story makes me thankful that our problems are not as bad as Job's. God often gives the most extreme examples in the Bible, so later readers like you and I can appreciate that there were others who experienced even worse than what we are experiencing. As rough as life possibly is for you and me, it was worse for Job in his hour of testing.

Job could not possibly have been prepared for a trial of this caliber, but he was prepared for just about anything else. He built up a significant nest egg and wisely distributed it into various investments. Just in case the sheep market plummeted, he would still have his camels and oxen and asses. You just never know when the price of sheep is going to fall on the ANE (Ancient Near-East) stocks and commodities exchange. But it wouldn't have mattered much to Job, because he made certain his investment portfolio was diversified.

Beyond preparing for himself, Job had even prepared for his children. Each day that his kids had a feast (which was likely every day of the week), Job offered sacrifices to God *for them.* Can you imagine going to confessional for the *possible* discrepancies of your *children*? Basically Job did just that. In his day, Job was not only *Mr. Ancient Near-East,* but he also might have held the regional title of "Mr. Prepared."

Maybe you also did *your* best to prepare for life's unexpected twists and turns. You thought you had enough savings set aside to retire. Or possibly you were just getting rid of your credit bills when the worldwide financial collapse caught you off-guard. Yet, the fact remains, when God decides to put you through a life-test, it doesn't matter how prepared you are. There is nobody on planet earth who has ever been completely ready for a full-scale pop-faith-test from God, because when God initiates one of these tests, He can wipe-out every preparation within a few mere minutes, as with Job.

Regardless, there is a good chance you have been condemned for your financial problems by your relatives and friends. After all, it hasn't happened to *them* (yet!), so they feel like they have the right to accuse you of wrongdoing. Job's wife and friends fit this bill. To be fair, they did not mean any harm; they just did not understand God's dealings in Job's life. They had never heard of a pop-faith-test, so they only offered the best advice they knew. Keep in mind, God did not inform *them* of Job's test, either. Similarly, you can't expect your family and friends to understand either. God hasn't informed them of your spiritual examination schedule, and they have never been through a similar pop-faith-test of this caliber on their own. Therefore, don't let their accusations of poor money management take root in your heart—that's the last thing you need right now.

The truth is, no matter where a person might stash-away their money, there is always a degree of uncertainty. It can all crash in the twinkling of an eye. Investing in stocks is a chance, because stock markets have been known to crash when all was thought to be safe. Real estate was thought to be a secure investment, until the "bubble" popped. Retirement pensions are almost a joke these days, as once-sound companies go under and then "reorganize" to rid themselves of "wasteful liabilities" (which includes retiree pensions). Savings accounts seem to be less risky, but banks have a bad habit of going bankrupt just when people need their money the most. Even the age-old method of hiding cash under the mattress isn't completely risk-free, as paper currency has been known to hyper-inflate and thereby loose nearly all of its value—other modern countries have experienced this tragedy. If this were to happen in America, a fistful of Ben Franklins might buy a loaf of bread.

As much as we try to fool ourselves into thinking otherwise, *there is absolutely no fool-proof investment anywhere in the world.* Nobody has sovereign control over our nation's monetary system, and therefore it is impossible for any of us to completely isolate ourselves from today's economic roller-coaster. Moreover, this is especially the case when God chooses to spring a pop-faith-test on you. To put it bluntly, *there is no safeguard against fire from heaven.* Job learned this the hard way, and maybe you have, too.

Job did not *expect* his life to crumble before his eyes. But it still did. You might feel like your life has been crumbling also, and it hurts badly. So, what do you do when life totally falls apart? There are several options. You could blame God. You could blame others. You could blame yourself. Or you could bury your head in the sand and cry. On Job's tragic day, he probably weighed each of these carefully. However, he chose a different, and unexpected, option . . . *he worshipped.* The Bible says, "Then Job arose, tore his robe, and shaved his head; and he fell to the ground and worshiped" (Job 1:20, NKJV). Right there on the spot he wrote and performed the oldest recorded Judeao-Christian worship song in existence today. It goes like this: "Naked I came from my mother's womb, and naked shall I return there. The LORD gave, and the LORD has taken away; blessed be the name of the LORD" (Job 1:21, NKJV). Then the Bible adds the commentary, "In all this Job did not sin nor charge God with wrong" (Job 1:22, NKJV).

Job had just begun the mother of all pop-faith-tests, and his response was perfect. You see, devotion to God is not tested when everything is going well. It's easy to follow God when life is peachy. However, God wants to prove to the watching world that you are going to follow Him even when those peaches become rotten and stinky. Job's response says volumes about his character. Honestly, I chose the two options of crying and blaming God when my test hurt the most. I wish I could say I was more spiritually mature back then, but I was not. When life hits hard, we typically revert to our most basic emotional responses.

Please understand, there is nothing wrong with crying, in fact it is an appropriate and emotionally-healing response. But to bury one's head in the sand in an attempt to ignore the situation is not helpful. Neither is blaming God or yourself or others. Although it is difficult, perhaps the best thing we can do during tough times is to put the rest of life on hold and simply *worship God*. If you are in a pop-faith-test, then this is the response God is looking for.

The point is, please don't make the mistake of blaming yourself when it happens. You see, no math instructor would give a calculus examination to a toddler. Likewise, God wouldn't have subjected you to the extreme test you are facing unless He was sure you could succeed at it. In fact, maybe God Himself was showing-off your faith just before your trials hit, just as He was with Job. Job was not privy to the conversation when God initiated a contest with Satan regarding Job's faithfulness: "Have you considered My servant Job, that *there is* none like him on the earth, a blameless and an upright man, one who fears God and shuns evil?" (Job 1:8, NKJV). And neither are you able to hear heaven's conversations about *you*, either. Maybe God was boasting about you just before your pop-faith-test hit! Even further, the Bible promises that God won't give you a test beyond your abilities (1 Corinthians 10:13); but this also means that God *will* give you tests which *will require* your full abilities. These will push you to your maximum limit. Besides, the test itself is proof enough that you are another one of God's prized possessions. *A test is not proof of your fault—it is evidence of your great faithfulness.*

I believe today's Christianity includes an inaccurate understanding of faith-tests. Many believers have been taught, in essence, that good things happen to good people, and bad things happen to sinful people. Therefore, when we see someone in the church going through a difficult faith-test, we automatically assume they brought it on themselves. Although this is *sometimes* the case, it is not *always* the case. Further, it is inconsistent with the way we perceive tests in all other areas of life. For some reason, the word "test" has taken on a completely different definition when it is applied to religious faith than the normal definition which is used for all other tests in life.

For example, if you would have walked down the hallway of my high school a dozen years ago and peeked into a classroom, you might have seen me sitting at a desk diligently working on a calculus examination (I took plenty of those). Would it have even occurred to you that I was sitting there taking a calculus test because I did something *wrong*? Certainly not! Instead, you would immediately think, "wow, he must be a *brilliant student* to be able to handle such a difficult test!" Well, "brilliant" is probably too strong of a word, but you get the point. If I hadn't gotten through several other tough math classes, I never would have been presented with a calculus test. If we stick with this normal understanding of the word *test*, then it must be admitted that we Christians are not tested in matters of faith because we did something *wrong*. Instead, we are subjected to such faith-tests because we did *so much right*.

The point is, don't let others blame you when things going awry. Your finances, or your health, or your child's issues are not your fault. God knows you did the very best job you could; this is all He expects from anybody. As with Job, God is simply using your life to prove to the watching world that His goodness goes beyond the material benefits which He sometimes gives. Job demonstrated this when he worshiped God after his trials.

Before we go any further, it is important to understand what God's contest over Job's faith was *really* about. In effect, it was focused on whether Job would curse God. This is found in Satan's response to God's second-round challenge: "Skin for skin! Yes, all that a man has he will give for his life. But stretch out Your hand now, and touch his bone and his flesh, and he will surely curse You to Your face!"(Job 2:4–5, NKJV).

You see, Satan believed that people will only serve God when He gives health and wealth. However, God was out to disprove this theory by demonstrating that no condition or circumstance would provoke Job to speak against his beloved God.

If the conditions of *your* contest were the same, would your response have given God the victory? To put it another way, what words have come from your mouth since life broadsided you? During hard times Christians are often tempted to blame God and question His goodness. This was exactly the point of God's contest with Satan. After all, if God is truly sovereign and in-charge, then why did these bad things happen? But it is important to remember that God's intention has never been to make you bitter with Him. He has nothing but good thoughts about you, and as the perfect Father, He will not provoke you to anger. In fact, he even expects human fathers to live up to this level of respect for their children, "Fathers, do not provoke your children, lest they become discouraged" (Colossians 3:21, NKJV). God is neither trying to anger you nor discourage you. He is, however, trying to use your life to accomplish much more than you probably know.

For quite some time now, your unbelieving neighbors and coworkers have known you are a Christian. From time to time they have wondered exactly why you attend church and serve God with your lifestyle. However, they have settled for the answer that you do these things as a type of "religious charm" to help make life go well for you. A Marine Corps Gunnery Sergeant I know might say that you follow God because He is your "sugar daddy." The idea is that God gives you "sugar-candy" (i.e., material blessings) in exchange for your obedience.

Your neighbors saw your ear to ear grin when you were "blessed" with a new car. At the time, you probably even bragged to them about how God *gave it to you*. They witnessed your praises for God at the birth of your children, and your heaven-directed thankfulness for your promotions at work. However, they've never seen you go through the junk everybody else goes through. They think your Jesus is nothing more than your *sugar daddy*. And now that your hard times have hit, those same neighbors and coworkers are watching you like a hawk to see how you react to your trials. *Only then* they will know if you are motivated by the *sugar*, or by the *Savior*. And this answer will tell them more about *God* than it tells them about *you*. This is about something more than your comfort; God's reputation in their eyes is at stake.

But don't think that this is simply about God preserving His reputation—there is much more at risk than that. The eternal destinies of your friends and family are at stake. Don't forget that today's financial crisis has not only affected you and me. It is an epidemic which has disrupted the lives of millions, including your neighbors and loved ones. They are feeling the same financial pain as you (maybe even worse), and if they see that Jesus can help you get through *your* tough times, then they just might be persuaded to let the Lord help *them* get through *their* tough times, too. It's great that the "light" of your Christian witness shines brightly in the good times, but be sure that it also shines brightly in the bad times. There is a lot more riding on it than you probably know.

After his first round of troubles, Job's light was still shining. He used his mouth to worship God instead of to curse God. This response gave both God *and Job* the victory in that first round. However, this instigated a second round in the heavenly match, again initiated by God. He boasted of Job just as in the first round, but then added, "And still he holds fast to his integrity, although you incited Me against him, to destroy him *without cause*" (Job 2:3, NKJV, emphasis added).

In recent years, Job has caught a lot of flack as people try to blame him for his trials in their attempt to support a predetermined theology. Usually Job is faulted for admitting to fear (as in Job 3:25). However, God clearly proclaims that there was nothing in Job which was cause for his test, except for his faithfulness. In fact, God Himself accepts the full responsibility for initiating it (Job 2:3)! Job wasn't given this faith-test because he had done something wrong; he was given the test because he had done everything *right*. In essence, God was showing-off His prize racehorse. The point is this: *only the best take the test.* Don't be ashamed of what you are going through. If you are like Job, then it is not your fault in the least. In fact, God is using your faith-test to show-off your prized devotion to Him, which is not something to be ashamed of. To the contrary, it is a *great honor.*

Satan upped the ante: "But stretch out Your hand now, and touch his bone and his flesh, and he will surely curse You to Your face!" (Job 2:5, NKJV). God obliged: "Behold, he *is* in your hand, but spare his life" (Job 2:6, NKJV). As the stakes for this second contest increased, Job's problems compounded. He was struck with boils all over his body, from the crown of his head to the tip of his toes (Job 2:7). Job had not only lost all of his family and possessions, but now he lost his health. Does the concept of multiple life problems resonate with you?

Major life issues rarely come in ones. Typically one significant problem makes a way for another, and another. For example, *health* problems alone can be devastating. But often the debilitating illness makes it impossible to earn a wage, which usually marks the onset of *financial* problems. Moreover, since the greatest cause for divorce is financial issues, *marriage* problems can quickly follow. Job experienced trials on all three of these fronts simultaneously.

With this round of multiple problems, Job did his best to keep his light shining. However, it was slightly dimmer. This time the Bible does not record that he worshiped God. Probably he no longer had the wherewithal to prostrate himself as before or sing his previous worship song. Maybe the pain from his boils prevented him from these things. Instead he picked up a piece of broken pottery and sat down and began to scrape his wounds for comfort.

As Job scraped his wounds, his wife gave him some less-than-godly advice about how he should handle his tragic situation: ". . . Curse God and die!" (Job 2:9, NKJV). Her proposed method for Job to find release from his problems and pain was to end his life. You also might have pondered similar thoughts inside your mind. Suicide might have begun looking like a realistic alternative to your suffering, but my friend, *please don't do it*. God is not angry with you, and this trial will not last forever. Please, find a counselor or a pastor who will speak words of encouragement into your life. You are created in the image of God, and you have so much more to offer this world than you realize.

By the time Ken Baldwin was 28 years old he suffered from severe depression. After listening to the voice of doom, he concluded that there were no possible solutions to his many problems. Suicide was the only answer. With this in mind, he strolled along the walking path of San Francisco's Golden Gate Bridge until he reached mid-span, 220-feet above the water. Worried his confidence might falter if he proceeded cautiously, he grabbed the four-foot high railing and vaulted himself clean over it. During his four-second fall he reached a speed of about 75 miles per hour, and then plunged feet-first into the bay. Since 1938 over 1,500 people have jumped from the Golden Gate Bridge; only 26 have survived. Ken was a lucky one. Rescuers pulled him from the icy-cold water with severe internal injuries. Later he was interviewed about his suicide attempt. He recalled watching his hand clear the railing, "I instantly realized that everything in my life that I'd thought was unfixable was totally fixable—except for having just jumped."[2]

Whatever you are going through is minor compared to suicide. If you have been contemplating this, please tell a friend, or a pastor, or someone else who truly cares for you and will help. Make it a point to stop listening to the awful voice of doom, despair, and destruction. Instead, spend time with God. Go to church, read your Bible, and talk with God in prayer. Life's difficulties are just God's invitations. I guarantee that God's highest priority is to convince you that your life is worth living.

Wisely, Job rejected this suicidal thought immediately and completely. He shot back at his wife, "You speak as one of the foolish women speaks. Shall we indeed accept good from God, and shall we not accept adversity?" (Job 2:10a, NKJV). The Bible then adds, "In all this Job did not sin with his lips" (Job 2:10b, NKJV). So, why was the specific focus of this challenge based on Job's words? Or, to ask it another way, why is it so important to honor God with our speech? After all, if someone were to curse God, wouldn't God just forgive them?

Of course God will forgive a person who sins against Him with their tongue. He has made provision for the forgiveness of these (and all) sins by the death of His Son Jesus Christ on the cross. However, even though God will forgive and forget, the watching world will not. Skeptics of the world are constantly watching, waiting to pounce on any Christian who would denounce God's goodness. Nonetheless, unbelievers are often won to Christ when they see true faithfulness in Christ's followers. This is why our common enemy Satan tries to push each of us into sin. Sin causes a disruption in our relationship with God, and even further, it ruins our credibility with people. Although sin can be forgiven and a disrupted relationship with God can be restored, the damage done to those watching might be nearly irreparable.

In addition, each of us has our own individual limits of how much pressure we can take. None of us knows our own personal limits, but God unquestionably does. This is partly why He gives different levels of tests to different people. For some, the short-term loss of a job might be their maximum limit for a pop-faith-test. Meanwhile another's faith really isn't tested until they lose their job *and* their home *and* their marriage. Although everybody will be given pop-faith-tests from time to time, the most difficult tests are reserved for God's toughest soldiers.

Job's faith was of the utmost depth and quality. Because of this, God knew that Job *could* and *would* pass the most difficult of all pop-faith-examinations. If another's difficulty seems *minor* compared to yours, please remember that it is still a major trial to *their* faith. If someone's difficulties appear *greater* than your own, don't give them the kind of advice that Job's friends gave him. Instead, pray for them, offer your friendship, and find a way to help them. After all, you may find yourself in a similar test one day and you would want someone on your side, also.

Job's test probably lasted for several months or more. The Bible spends thirty-four more chapters depicting the doctrinal exchanges between Job and his three or four friends. Job's complaint can be summarized by this portion from one of his discourses:

> Look, I go forward, but He is not *there*, and backward, but I cannot perceive Him; when He works on the left hand, I cannot behold *Him*; when He turns to the right hand, I cannot see *Him*. But he knows the way that I take; *when* He has tested me, I shall come forth as gold. My foot has held fast to his steps; I have kept His way and not turned aside. I have not departed from the commandment of His lips; I have treasured the words of His mouth more than my necessary *food*. But He *is* unique, and who can make Him change? And *whatever* His soul desires, that He does. For He performs *what is* appointed for me (Job 23:8–14a, NKJV).

From this we understand that Job felt separated from God's presence. If you are going through a pop-faith-test, then you probably feel this isolation, also. This is normal. Remember, the professor does not help the test-taker during the test. Nonetheless, God did not *really* separate Himself from Job; it only *seemed* as if He did. If you feel isolated from God, remember—*it is only a feeling*. If you are a Christian, the Lord Jesus Christ has already promised to be with you forever (Matthew 28:20). Nothing can separate you from God, regardless of how you feel.

Further, Job understood his trials were temporary and purposeful. It is dangerous to accept the idea that our trials are purposeless. As long as we recognize that God has a purpose for our difficulties, we can find a way to get through them. Moreover, when we realize that tests are a temporary situation rather than a permanent condition, we understand that we have a bright future to look forward to.

We also learn that Job understood he could only "pass" his pop-faith-test if he remained faithful to God. Job realized that some things in life one *cannot* change (like his circumstances and God's actions in his life), but other things in life one *can* change (like his reactions and his speech). The same rings true with you and me. There are many aspects of our situations which we *cannot* change, but we are *in-control* of our reactions and responses to those difficulties. And you can choose to do what is right, regardless of your situation. *Don't lose your faith during your faith-test.* God rewards all those who endure (see Hebrews 12:10). I cannot promise that God will grant your specific request if you remain faithful to Him. However, you can be sure He will *not* grant your request if you *do not* remain faithful.

I hope you will take the time to read the entire book of Job, but at the very least I invite you to read God's response to Job in chapters 38–42. It is well worth the time. In the end, God completely restored Job: "Now the LORD blessed the latter *days* of Job more than his beginning" (Job 42:12a, NKJV). He received twice the number of his original sheep, camels, oxen, and donkeys (Job 42:12). Further, God gave Job ten more children (including ten more *childbirths* possibly to reward Job's wife for her bad advice), adding an additional blessing of staggering beauty to his three daughters (Job 42:13–15). And in Job's personal life, God granted him another 140 years to enjoy the fruits of life (Job 42:16).

The principle here is this: *God lavishly rewards His people for faithfully enduring trials.* If you are like Job, then your trials are only a pop-faith-test to prove that God is much more than the "sugar daddy" which many people make Him out to be. Even in your darkest moment you are not alone; the Lord Jesus Christ is right there with you. It may seem as if God will never rescue you . . . but He will. Remember, your trial is only temporary, so remain faithful to God in your words and in your actions. And if you will continue to honor God through your test, then like Job, you also will "come forth like gold!" (Job 23:10, NET) *Guaranteed.*

Discussion Questions

1. What is a "pop-faith-test," and are Christians today subjected to pop-faith-tests? What might a test like this look like?

2. Does a faith-test alter our *actual relationship* with God? Why or why not?

3. What trials did Job face? Was Job guilty of having not properly prepared for difficulties?

4. Is there any way to become financially protected from God's pop-tests? Why or why not?

5. How did Job react to his trials? What do his responses tell us about Job?

6. How have you responded to your trials? What can you learn about yourself from your responses, and what would it look like if you reacted to your own trials as Job did?

7. Are times of testing based upon one's fault, or one's faithfulness? Why?

8. Who is watching you go through your trials? How can your response to difficulties affect their lives for the better?

9. Who can you talk to if you have contemplated suicide recently? Do you know anybody who might be considering suicide? How can you help them?

10. What important truths does someone need to know while they are going through pop-faith-tests?

11. How did Job's story end? What kind of hope does this give you?

3

Somebody Else Got Me Into This Mess

Paul (Part A): Sailing into Life's Storms

(Acts 27:1–38)

A religious hope does not only bear up the mind
under her sufferings but makes her rejoice in them.

—Joseph Addison

I f you want to sail the Caribbean Sea you have two choices: you can
purchase a ticket aboard a cruise ship, or you can join the U.S. Coast
Guard. I spent three years as a "Coastie," during which time I patrolled
the Caribbean waters often. When my medium-sized cutter stopped for
fuel at Tortolla, St. Maarten, or Antigua, it was sometimes docked be-
side a passenger liner. So I can assure you that if the Caribbean is your
goal, both methods will get you there equally well, and both agencies
are eager for your involvement. However, before you hunt the internet
for a cruise ticket, or speed-off to enlist at a military recruiting station
it might be worth your time to consider a few minor distinctions with
these competing agencies.

  With the cruise ship you will choose the ports you visit and the
dates you travel. But the Coast Guard knows these decisions can be
daunting, so they relieve you of that burden; the Government chooses
for you. A typically passenger liner will ask you to leave after only one
week of cruising. Meanwhile, the USCG permits you to remain onboard
for up to two months! The bulky cruise ship is nearly 1,200 feet long
and avoids rough weather to ensure your trip is bathed in monotony. In

contrast, the Coast Guard knows a dash of excitement will enhance your Caribbean experience, so they built their small and agile vessel to be a cure for boredom as it *chases* storms.

Maybe the better choice is becoming clearer to you. Just in case it is not, permit me to explain some more. If your health is a concern (and let's face it, today *everybody* is concerned), then the Coast Guard is the right choice for you. The CG has a pre-cruise physical exercise "camp" to help travelers set and meet fitness goals. Meanwhile the passenger ship's apparent goal is to enable each person to *roll* ashore at port calls. Furthermore, cruise ships require you to award monies to them, while the Coast Guard monetarily rewards *you* for choosing to sail aboard their vessel. The Coast Guard will even provide your wardrobe for the passage. At this point the choice should be quite clear. And it is amazing that cruise lines remain in business with such brilliant competition! (By the way, don't forget to mention my name at the recruiting station).

All joking aside, the most significant difference between these two groups is found in their *missions*. The purpose of cruise lines is to provide a high-quality sailing experience for vacationers. Meanwhile, one main mission of the Coast Guard is to save lives at sea. With a cruise ship you will enjoy comfort and relaxation at sea. With the Coast Guard you will work hard to save lives. *Va*-cation versus *vo*-cation: big difference.

The truth is God has not called His people to a *va*-cation, but to a *vo*-cation. Our overarching duty in life is to reach others for Christ regardless of where we find ourselves or what we find ourselves doing. Certainly there will be periods of R&R (rest and relaxation), however the primary duty of a Christian is not to be *"livin' the life"* of affluence and leisure. Instead, it is to *labor* in God's vineyard of lost people. Sometimes we find ourselves expecting life to be as comfortable and accommodating as a cruise liner, and we can get discouraged when it doesn't work-out this way for us. But God has no vacation vessels. He only has vocation ships with workers onboard like you and me. We are indeed sailing through life, but we are not *passengers*. The Bible makes it clear that we are *workers* as the Apostle Paul instructs, "Therefore, my beloved brethren, be steadfast, immovable, always abounding in the work of the Lord, knowing that your labor is not in vain in the Lord" (1 Corinthians 15:58, NKJV).

So when we find ourselves in one of life's storms we should not be surprised (1 Peter 4:12–13). It is normal for life-saving vessels to go into messy situations to find and save those in danger—this is their *purpose*. Likewise, it is normal for Christians to be in the messy world to reach people—this is *our* purpose. If you were to encounter no storms in life, I might even question the reality of your Christian experience. All those in God's service find themselves in the storms of life periodically. Even the great Apostle Paul did. Although his was a literal storm in the Mediterranean Sea, we can glean much truth from his experience.

The Apostle Paul had been arrested and was on the way to his hearing before Caesar Augustus in Rome. To get there he was chained to a Roman Centurion soldier named Julius who would escort him on the approximate 2,000-mile trip, mostly to be travelled at sea. After their first leg of the journey Julius booked their passage on a ship going towards Rome. This is where we pick up the story, in Acts 27:

> We came to a place called Fair Havens, near the city *of* Lasea. Now when much time had been spent, and sailing was now dangerous because the Fast was already over, Paul advised them, saying, "Men, I perceive that this voyage will end with disaster and much loss, not only of the cargo and ship, but also our lives." Nevertheless the centurion was more persuaded by the helmsman and the owner of the ship than by the things spoken by Paul. And because the harbor was not suitable to winter in, the majority advised to set sail from there also, if by any means they could reach Phoenix, a harbor of Crete opening toward the southwest and northwest, *and* winter *there*. When the south wind blew softly, supposing that they had obtained *their* desire, putting out to sea, they sailed close by Crete (Acts 27:8b-13, NKJV).

Paul had been doing God's will, no doubt about it. He had preached the Gospel of the risen Savior to the Jews in Jerusalem, and to several high-level Roman officials and military officers, and now he was on his way to deliver God's message to Caesar himself. God had already informed Paul that he would bring this message of life and hope to Rome (Acts 23:11). There is absolutely no mistaking the fact that Paul was smack-dab in the middle of God's will for his life.

There was, however, a slight dilemma. Should they sail forty miles to winter at the protective harbor at the port of Phoenix, or should they remain in Fair Havens although it was less suitable for wintering? Paul volunteered his insight: "If we go, the ship will lose the cargo and we'll probably all lose our lives" (Acts 27:10, paraphrased). They probably called Paul crazy, or at the very least they called him an ignorant pessimist. After all, what did a religious fanatic know about sailing, anyway? Then the accommodating winds came, and the decision was made: they set sail. What others saw as *opportunity*, Paul saw as *catastrophe*. A journey which should have lasted a half-day would quickly become the ordeal of a lifetime. Is the theme-song to *Gilligan's Island* coming to mind right about now?

We're going to pause here for a brief logic-check. First point: God wanted Paul to get to Rome *alive*. Second point: according to Paul's divine insight, the ship that Julius wanted to take was going to be lost along with the lives of all onboard. So, logically we would expect God to intervene and *somehow* keep Paul out of this dilemma, right? Maybe God would subtly convince Julius to wait-out the winter in Fair Havens. Or God might have even stopped the wind from blowing, which would have kept the whole ship in port. At any rate, God had several *logical* options which would have kept Paul off a doomed ship. However, God chose to do none of them.

Instead, the Roman soldier trusted the ship owner and helmsman over Paul; the experience of two seasoned sailors outweighed the advice of one "religious nut"—who could blame him? The wind blew just right, and the ship set sail. Here we learn our first principle from this story: *God does not operate according to our logic.* Out of the many ways the Lord *could have* intervened, instead, He chose to *not* intervene. Everybody in the ship (including Paul) was left at the mercy of the sea, and ultimately, to the fate which Paul had described. Knowing this, we can now expect things to get pretty messy in Paul's life: "But not long after, a tempestuous head wind arose, called Euroclydon. So when the ship was caught, and could not head into the wind, we let *her* drive" (Acts 27:14–15, NKJV).

It typically takes an extended period of time for circumstances to go from bad to good; but they can go from good to bad in the blink of an eye. This is exactly what happened in Paul's case as "Euroclydon" arrived. In Paul's day, Euroclydon was known for being so fierce that it struck fear into the hearts of even the most experienced sailors. It is no coincidence that the actual Greek word used here to describe this wind sounds conspicuously similar to "typhoon." And if you have spent time at sea, or near a sea coast, then you know the terror which strikes at the mention of this word.

Forward progress for the vessel was impossible because of this headwind. So they had the option to lower the ship's sails and attempt to remain motionless in the water (and likely face capsizing from broadside waves and swells), or keep the sails up and go in the opposite direction. They chose to keep-up the sails, spin around, and "let *her* drive" (Acts 27:15, NKJV). Basically, they fastened the ship's wheel to keep her at full speed, and with no idea of where they were going, they *hoped for the best*. This is similar to closing your eyes while driving at highway speed, and *hoping* to stay on the road. In the world of sailing it is *dangerous*.

It might feel like this is what is happening with your finances, too. With the economy spinning out of control, there seems to be no stability for any of us. Some economists expect a quick turn-around of America's financial woes, but that's only because they still have their jobs. Take away their lavish salaries and they will sing a different song. For those of us who have lost our jobs (including me) there is only a tunnel with no light. And it is downright frightening to be at the mercy of a financial storm.

Regarding Paul, we must accept that his life was not in danger because of something *he* did. No, the reason for his awful situation was because of something the *Roman Centurion* did. This same thing may apply to you and me. If you are going through "h-e-double-hockey-sticks" on earth, it is not necessarily your fault. Paul was literally in a life-and-death situation because of *somebody else's* bad decision, and it might be the same with you. Paul duly warned his guard, giving him the inside scoop on the outcome, but Julius did not listen. Yet, still the apostle was dragged onboard before he could say "keep me off that sinking ship."

I spent almost an entire year feeling like God was mad at me, and accepting the blame for feeling this way. I mistakenly thought that since my suffering was not a direct result of witnessing efforts, it must some-how be self-induced. And I couldn't figure-out what I was doing wrong! I tried to be as obedient and as faithful to the Lord Jesus as I could, but my financial problems persisted. I had been taught that God's will for the Christian was a neat and tidy life which fit inside a neat and tidy box and was tied-up with a neat and tidy ribbon. It was to be a life without difficulties, hardship, or suffering. Yet my life was anything *but* this.

Therefore, I had no other choice but to think I had committed some mysterious sin for which I was being punished, and I only had myself to blame. It was in the midst of this struggle when I learned a tremendous lesson from Paul: *everything which enters the Christian's life has already gone through the "God-filter."* Regardless of what you are going through, just like with Paul, God has allowed it . . . *all* of it (even if it was because of somebody else's bad decision).

If you desire to follow Jesus and are trying to do so, then God is pleased with you, and with your faithful perseverance. As we have already seen, this is the whole point of the book of Job, and the reason why God put it in the Biblical cannon, never to be removed from the Bible, or from our church theologies. If our theology does not include the presence of the arbitrary suffering of Christians, then that theology is not true to the entirety of the Bible and needs to be revised.

Just as the absence of problems cannot implicate one's innocence, *the presence of problems cannot implicate one's guilt.* In fact, the strongest biblical evidence of the apostolic calling is suffering (see 1 Corinthians 4:9). You certainly would not have found Paul staying in a 5-star Roman hotel! So unless God Himself convicts you of sin, you are to follow Paul's example and hold your head up high because you are a royal servant, doing God's bidding. You may not be aware of the intricacies involved in bringing you into your dire circumstances, but you can rest assured that you are a beloved child of the most-high God, and He is *always* watching over you. Moreover, if you are like Paul, then your problems are only there because of your calling and devotion to Him. Paul was subject to significant tribulation throughout his life because of his faithfulness to his calling. Take a look at the short list of Paul's difficulties:

> From the Jews five times I received forty *stripes* minus one. Three times I was beaten with rods; once I was stoned [nearly to death!]; three times I was shipwrecked; a night and a day I have been in the deep; *in* journeys often, *in* perils of waters, *in* perils of robbers, *in* perils of *my own* countrymen, *in* perils of the Gentiles, *in* perils in the city, *in* perils in the wilderness, *in* perils in the sea, *in* perils among false brethren; in weariness and toil, in sleeplessness often, in hunger and thirst, in fastings often, in cold and nakedness—besides the other things, what comes upon me daily: my deep concern for all the churches (2 Corinthians 11:24–28, NKJV).

The sad fact is, when a believer *does* go through honest struggles, more often than not they receive accusation instead of honest friendship and support from their fellow Christians. They are treated as second-class believers who carry a rare but contagious strain of an ancient plague of poverty. If you doubt this, I challenge you to take a look around your own church. You have probably hardly even noticed the older divorced woman who doesn't dress quite so nicely. The divorce wasn't her fault; nobody knew she was marrying an abusive man. Yet it has affected every moment of her life since. She arrives at church late to avoid the discomfort of feeling lonely while everyone else is mingling. If you expect to see her socializing after the sermon you will be disappointed. People pass her on their way down the aisle, but none stop to really talk with her. She is a barrier to go around, not an individual to seek. To most she is not important enough to remember her name, or even make eye-contact. So she quietly finds her way to the side-door of the church, and ambles to her car. Nobody notices when she's there, and nobody notices when she's gone. And at the safety of her home she'll relieve the pain by crying herself to sleep.

Although we would never say it, people treat her as a second-class Christian. I know this because she's not only in your church; she is in mine, too. In fact, you can find her and, others like her, in any church. It is a shameful truth that she could probably find more support and consolation inside a bar than inside a church. At church nobody will go out of their way to associate with her. That is, nobody but Jesus. He is honored to be her Friend. The same is true with you. If others shy away from you, then you are closer to God than you could imagine. He is a friend to the lonely, and is always anxious to talk with you.

On the other hand, if your tribulations are the result of your involvement in sin, then please don't think that God is finished with you. The Lord will fully restore you to the community of believers again. While Israel wandered in the wilderness for forty years, sometimes a repentant transgressor was immediately restored to service inside the camp. Other times, however, the repentant offender was kept outside the camp for a season to be mended before they were allowed to return to the community. It all depended upon the offense and the depth to which it affected others in the community. The same is true today. So if you find yourself "outside the camp," do not give-up on yourself, because God has not given-up on you. Continue being faithful to your Lord, and He will restore you when the time is right.

> And running under *the shelter of* an island called Clauda, we secured the skiff with difficulty. When they had taken it on board, they used cables to undergird the ship; and fearing lest they should run aground on the Syrtis *Sands*, they struck sail and so

were driven. And because we were exceedingly tempest-tossed, the next *day* they lightened the ship. On the third *day* we threw the ship's tackle overboard with our own hands. Now when neither sun nor stars appeared for many days, and no small tempest beat on *us*, all hope that we would be saved was finally given up (Acts 27:16–20, NKJV).

The crew of Paul's vessel undergirded the hull with thick ropes to support the creaking, groaning structure. The vessel was probably filling with water, making it necessary to throw-off cargo and all other necessary weight in order to stay afloat. At this point, the safety of the ship became infinitely more important than even the preservation of its cargo. They even lowered their sails to keep the hull and rigging intact, although it would make the vessel even more vulnerable to capsizing. These steps probably helped, but they did not resolve their problems nor restore their hope. Without the benefit of seeing the sun or stars, they had absolutely no idea where they were. It is a rare instance in life when any further attempt to stop a disaster is futile. But for Paul's crew, this was one of those times. The situation was so bad that these experienced sailors actually gave up all hope of surviving this storm.

The problem with storms at sea is they last for *so very long*. There is almost nothing to slow the wind or waves, so they keep going—seemingly forever. This is especially hard on those of us who are prone to sea-sickness. Do you remember the amusement park ride which made you nauseous when you were younger (you might have even lost your lunch after riding it)? If you can imagine staying on that ride nonstop for three days, then you can imagine what a harsh storm at sea is like. On the ocean storms don't just come and go within a few hours like they often do on land. A vessel will feel the effects of a sizeable storm for several days or more. Experienced sailors jokingly say there are two stages of seasickness. The first stage is when you become so sick that you are afraid that you just might *die*. But if the storm persists you will eventually enter stage two, when you become so sick that you become afraid that you just might *live*.

If it seems like your storm is lasting forever, you might have to follow these sailors' example, and "undergird" your financial ship. Make whatever adjustments or changes that need to be made. Stop frivolous spending. Clip coupons and buy generic. Eat P-B-and-J . . . lots of it. Take Dave Ramsey's *Financial Peace University* class; we did and it helped my wife and I get our finances in order. When you only have one ship, you must do *everything in you power* to keep it floating. If you are going through something similar, then you know exactly what I am talking about. In addition, you also understand what Paul went through in his storm. However, God was not about to let Paul's hope of preaching before Caesar die in the waves.

> But after long abstinence from food, then Paul stood in the midst of them and said, "Men, you should have listened to me, and not have sailed from Crete and incurred this disaster and loss. And now I urge you to take heart, for there will be no loss of life among you, but only of the ship. For there stood by me this night an angel of the God to whom I belong and whom I serve, saying, 'Do not be afraid, Paul; you must be brought before Caesar; and indeed God has granted you all those who sail with you.' Therefore take heart, men, for I believe God that it will be just as it was told me" (Acts 27:21–25, NKJV).

Paul finally spoke-up and appealed to the accuracy of his earlier advice. He then continued to deliver a message given him by an angel of God: Paul's appointment with Caesar had not been cancelled, and all 276 people (275 plus Paul) onboard would be spared. God had more usefulness for the apostle than to let him perish at sea. This insight energized Paul's optimism. And just as God would not let Paul (or his hope) die in the waves, neither will God let *your* hope die in *your* storm. Trust me: if God were finished with you on earth, He *knows* how to get you to your heavenly home, and I mean *right now*. Therefore, you can count every one of your breaths as proof that God still has more plans for your life.

While I was growing-up, my grandmother lived with my family, which made us quite close with her. My siblings and I jokingly called her "Groovy-Gra-Gra" because of her exceptional health and vitality, and also her wonderful sense of humor. When she was ninety-years old she broke her hip and had to have it surgically replaced. She spent weeks in the hospital recovering, teetering on the brink of death. One day my mother sat by her side while grandma's breathing and her heart both stopped. Alarms sounded and nurses arrived within a minute. But by then her breathing had resumed and her heart was beating again. Finding nothing wrong they left the room, and Groovy told my mother what happened.

She said it was like a dream; she stood at a stream and watched a distant figure walk towards her. She intuitively knew it was the Lord Jesus Christ. "Are you thirsty?" He asked. Parched, grandma nodded. He cupped his hands in the stream and lifted the pure water to her lips. She looked into His nail-holes as she drank. He asked, "Do you want to stay here, or do you want to go back?" She said she wanted to stay. He replied, "You must go back . . . there is more work for you to do." Then she woke-up again in the hospital bed, with alarms ringing and nurses swarming.

To me the truly amazing part of this story is my grandmother's age. Imagine: when my grandmother was *ninety-years old* (and stuck in a hospital bed), the Lord told her she had *more work to do* on earth. For five more years she did this "work," but it did not include preaching at evangelistic crusades. She did not lead a Bible study, attend seminary, or even read through the entire Bible again. Instead, she simply told people that God loved them and that she loved them, too. I can only suppose that by the end of those five years, Groovy-Gra-Gra had finished her work. Then the Lord brought her to her heavenly home for keeps.

If God had more work for my ninety-year-old hospitalized grandmother, then He definitely has work for *you*, also. God probably won't ask you to reach a warring tribe in the Amazon, but He *will* ask you to reach-out to your estranged coworkers, family, and friends. There are people you already know (and have yet to meet) who are in need of what you have to give. They might need your friendship, your blessing, or your acceptance. There are amends to be made, forgiveness to give, and loved ones to reclaim and embrace. There is *always* more work to be done. In addition, most of God's work is not done in stadium-sized events. It is accomplished in the daily interactions of personal relationships, and you can start wherever you find yourself. Paul did.

Another important lesson to take from this story is the old saying: *things are not always what they appear.* At the beginning of this voyage everybody else saw opportunity, except Paul—he saw devastation. However, by this point in their ordeal everybody else saw *doom*, but Paul saw *hope.* As believers in Jesus Christ we cannot afford to look at the outward appearance of our situations. We must view our circumstances through the eyes of faith in God. Things may seem to be going terribly in our own lives, just like things seemed awful for Paul. But the truth is we don't know *half* the story.

There is a master plan, a grand design for your life which you cannot see from the inside. You are truly a blessing to others, and you have so much more to offer. *The world needs what you have to give.* However, you must have God's outside perspective to truly understand your place and your importance in the world. If you want to see life from God's view, just ask Him. He's not hiding it. In fact, God would *rather* have you view life through His lens. Ask, and God will make you aware of your gifts and talents, and He will let you know how you can use them to purposefully advance His kingdom.

Earlier, nobody would listen to Paul, but after two weeks (see Acts 27:27) of being punished by typhoon-level winds and waves they were softened to the point of accepting counsel from their local "religious nut." Their training, skill, and expertise had finally been exhausted, and they had no other hope in the world. Now *Paul's* hope would become *their* hope. You see, this voyage was not just about Paul. We have empathized about Paul's unpleasant experience in this journey, but for the first time we now see that God's plan encompassed so much more than Paul alone. God was not concerned about Paul's *comfort*; He was concerned about Paul's *companions*.

God had a plan for each person aboard that doomed vessel, and it included softening them to the point of heeding Paul's words and honoring Paul's God. Paul strategically used every situation for his purpose of advancing the Gospel because he saw God's hand in all of his circumstances, even the really bad ones. In essence, the 275 crew and passengers on this ship were so important to God that He arranged for an apostle to go through a horrible storm to personally deliver the message of Jesus Christ at precisely the moment when their hearts were most ready to listen. Wow! If we could only begin to see our own lives in this light, we would better understand *our own* purpose in life.

Unless we are intentionally rebellious against God's leading in our lives (as Jonah was), our storms (or even shipwrecks) are not the result of personal wrongdoing. Nor are they an indication that God is unable to guide us around them, or unwilling to stop them. Paul was intent on getting to Rome, but he did not make the mistake of mislabeling this storm as a "delay" in God's plan for his life. Paul understood that he was on a mission which would deeply affect *every single person* aboard his ship. He also realized this storm was God's way of presenting him with a tremendous opportunity. Which brings us to our next truth: *storms are opportunities to overcome.*

While we seem to be ever-consumed with our future, God is already highly active and intricately involved in our *present.* We become busy preparing for God's plans for our *future,* and often don't even notice God's involvement in our *present.* As we rush to get to our appointments and meetings on time, any delay by traffic or friends or supermarket lines we label as an *interruption.* Yet we rarely appreciate that the detour *is* God's immediate plan. Sure, the "big things" in life will eventually come, but God wants to use us as agents of change wherever we are— even grocery store lines. If you want to know what God wants you to do in life, just look around. You will quickly notice somebody who needs what ministry you have to give, even if it is nothing more than a smile or a kind word. This is your *opportunity.*

Paul rarely let an opportunity go to waste, and this particular opportunity included God "giving" Him the lives of all those onboard. Paul was surrounded by 275 people who were about to lose their lives—275 people who needed a touch from God. And for two weeks God used this most trying ordeal to prepare them for that *one touch* when God would prove His love for each of them. In addition, the fact that God "granted" Paul these 275 indicates that Paul had already been praying that God would preserve their lives (see Acts 27:24, NKJV). In other words, *God gave Paul that which he had been petitioning for: the lives of all onboard.*

However, I believe it goes even deeper. I think God went one step beyond physical salvation and granted them *spiritual* salvation. It was not merely about *preserving their lives* (as if that were not enough); it was about *saving their souls.* And if Paul wasn't trapped in their sinking ship with them, they would have lost *both.*

My question for you is: who are your "275"? Who are the "shipmates" stuck in your storm with you? Surely you don't think you're the *only one* going through calamity, do you? There must be dozens, possibly even hundreds around you who are feeling the same pressures as you. It is fine if you want to pray for your own circumstances to improve, but you would be missing a tremendous opportunity if you did not pray for your own *275,* as well. Their lives are being ravished even more than yours, because you have Jesus Christ to give you some measure of stabilize and hope. *They don't.* Those around you have *nothing* to anchor their lives to. While you go to church and trust God for hope, they stare at their medicine cabinet deliberating how to end the pain of life.

You see, your comfort is *not* God's chief concern right now . . . their life and salvation *is*. God's intent is to touch their lives with the pure hope which only He can give, and there is nobody in a better position to present this hope to them than you. This is *your opportunity* to be a change-agent in the world of those around you. Don't let it slip away by becoming over-consumed with your problems. People need the message of hope which is tucked away in your heart. *Pray for them* when they don't think they need you, and *be there for them* when they realize they do.

Please understand, when the going gets tough is not the time to abandon your devotional life. It is a time to increase your face-time with God. A 10–15 minute devotional might be sufficient to keep you going strong each day during the "fat years." But when the "lean years" arrive you will need much more time on your knees to sustain your own hope, and still have enough to distribute to others.

Amazingly, Paul was ready to be God's instrument to touch lives *even in the midst of* this horrendous ordeal. Those two weeks of anguish shook 275 people (including hardened sailors) to their very cores, but it did not affect Paul's mental and emotional faculties in the least. In fact, he *overcame* his circumstances. Throughout the two-week ordeal he not only remained completely sane, but he was spiritually strong enough to minister to those around him. If I spent two weeks in a typhoon I might not even be able to *speak,* much less minister in love. But because of Paul's faith, he *did*. So, how did he do it? Well, certainly not by yielding to the temptation to panic, like so many of us today would. We do not find Paul running down the deck of the ship screaming, "We're all going to die!"

Instead, Paul acted in wisdom. He resisted the temptation to focus on mere self-survival, choosing rather to nurture his relationship with Jesus Christ. This gave him the much-needed stability, perspective, and purpose which everyone else onboard was lacking. Still today we are tempted to focus on personal survival, just like the rest of the crowd. Yet, if we will foster our relationship with the Lord, we would learn that God has more on His mind than just survival . . . He's thinking *multiplication*! You see, it is a "good deal" whenever God can use an ugly storm to turn one Christian into 276 Christians. That's a 27,500-percent return on investment, just because of the addition of *one* storm! You see, the storm was not the problem; the storm was the *solution*. The *crew* (or more specifically, the crew's resistance to Paul's message about God) was the *problem*. God wanted to *reach* those people. So, Paul had to understand his purpose and overcome the fear of death, in order to accomplish the mission of reaching his *275* with God's love. This is what being an *overcomer* is all about!

You might be stuck in your own sinking-ship situation with an ornery group who you never intended to go down with. It probably was not your idea, and it certainly was not your fault. But make no mistake, *God did allow it*. Even further, you must realize the storm is not your *problem*. The lack of faith of the people around you is the problem . . . the storm is your *solution,* and theirs. You have been praying for your family, friends, and coworkers, and this storm is just what they needed to bring them to the point of considering what you have to say. God has granted your request; don't blow it now by reacting in panic! You are the only person *on the planet* who has the position, the ability, and the will to reach them with God's love. Use this as your opportunity to finally break-into their lives with God's love and light. It will probably be difficult for you, just as it was for Paul. However, God did not place you in this position to fail; He placed you there to *succeed*. And with His help you *will* succeed. Continue to pray for your *275*, and be there for them. Soon they will need you.

I never pressed Christianity on my fellow sailors aboard ships, but they would inevitably discover my religious inclinations. Onboard one vessel there was a shipmate who made me the butt of his daily religious jokes. When others were not around he was pleasant towards me, but during meals and break times, religious slurs were his discussion of choice. Although I prayed for him, it was difficult to endure those public assaults. This went on for months. Then one day he confided in me that he had just learned his wife had filed for divorce. He was powerless in the situation, as we were at sea. This was *his* breaking point. He asked me to pray for his marriage, and we bowed our heads, prayed, and wept together. I was certain it did no good, and shortly afterwards we both left the ship for new assignments.

We ran into each other months later, and he gave me a joyful update. To my complete amazement, *God had saved his marriage*! His eyes gleamed as he described how his wife cried as she repented to him, and asked if he would still have her. It was amazing! Through that personal storm God proved Himself to this man, and today he still follows Jesus Christ. I am happy to say we have been friends ever since we bowed together in prayer, and he has often thanked me for helping him find God during that dark storm of his life. In reality it wasn't that he found God in his storm, but that God loved him enough to use the storm to break into his life. Moreover, my personal opportunity-cost was to simply endure some bad jokes. If this is all it takes to reach others, I'll gladly endure more bad jokes.

Likewise, your dire circumstances are not meant to discourage you, but to disrupt the intense hostility which those around you have towards God. God only messes with those who He loves, and He loves your 275 too much to *not* mess with their lives. In your situation, God's goal is to break everybody *but* you. Even if your storm still continues to rage out of control, do not give-up. This only means there are still more people to reach.

One common theme in the Bible is for God to send an emissary (usually one of His precious children) to those without hope. In your own situation, God loves your own troubled friends and coworkers so much that He sent . . . (drum-roll please) . . . *you. You* are God's instrument of grace to reach them, and sometimes life can get tough with a mission this grand. So don't think your problem is all about you. More likely it is all about *them.* And no matter what, *don't give-up.* Persist through your trying times and God will reach others through you.

You may be stuck in your situation, feeling every wave of financial setback with everyone else, but you are not forced to react in panic as they do. *Act in wisdom, and stay focused on God.* He will help you and He will come through for you. He always does. Only He can give you the stability and perspective you need to overcome the situation. Even further, only God can reveal to you your vital purpose of expanding His kingdom. God has arranged for your success by giving you the opportunity to reach-out to those around you. They might have considered you to be a religious nut before, but soon they will gladly listen to you. *Pray for them* when they want nothing to do with you, and *be there for them* when they have nowhere else to turn. And whatever you do, *don't lose heart*; this storm is your *opportunity to overcome!*

Discussion Questions

1. What is the difference between a spiritual vacation and a spiritual vocation? To which one are we, as Christians, called to?

2. The author stated "God does not operate according to our logic." What simple, logical solutions could God enact to put an end to your personal difficulties? Can you think of any reasons why God would *not* act upon these solutions? (For example, what other possibly higher priorities might God have in your situation?)

3. Is it possible that your trials are the result of somebody else's bad decisions? How so?

4. Why should you not feel ashamed of your circumstances?

5. Do you know anybody who reminds you of the lonely divorced woman in this chapter? What practical things could you do to become a better friend to him or her?

6. If you are in financial struggles, what practical adjustments can you make to "undergird" your financial ship?

7. Does God have more work for you to do in life? What work might this be?

8. Do you consider your current situation a *problem* or an *opportunity*? What would it take for you to see it as an opportunity?

9. Taking into account the entire scope of your situation, what is God's highest priority: your comfort or your companions?

10. Who are your "275," and how can you best help them?

4

I Lost Everything

Paul (Part B): God Orchestrates Your Shipwrecks

(ACTS 27:26–28:10)

What seems to us as bitter trials are often blessings in disguise.

—OSCAR WILDE

M Y "PERFECT STORM" BEGAN in the summer of 2007. But it wasn't
at sea . . . it was at *seminary*. My wife and I had agreed to move
into student housing to finish my last year of seminary, and meanwhile,
sell our condominium-home. At the time, the local real estate market
was at its peak. It seemed to be the perfect time to sell a condo located
two-blocks from the beach. We moved into student housing to make
room to renovate our home, and accomplished all the work ourselves.
By the time we were finished it looked immaculate, and seemed poised
for a lightning-fast sale. I proudly planted our "For Sale" sign in the front
yard on the Fourth of July 2007, and we waited. Then we waited some
more. The real estate "bubble" popped, and the condo would not sell. My
storm had begun.

We began with high hopes that our beautiful condo would sell. But
our hope eroded just as quickly as buyer confidence did. Each day without an offer was like another cold wave of harsh reality splashing over us.
We feared perishing in the storm of the collapsing housing market. Our
realtor warned it would only get worse, and he was right. Even fewer
buyers meant we were all but certain to lose our home. As the months
passed and our savings trickled away, all hope was finally gone. Then the

bank shifted the conversation from the subject of back-payments to that of foreclosure. This storm was going to cost me my career in the ministry before it even began, since no church would hire a pastor with a credit score in the double digits. My dream of a ministry career was over before it really even began. I had no hope left.

During these long months a friend gave me some advice: "just try to get through *today*. And when you wake-up tomorrow morning, try to do it *just one more time*." This ridiculously simple advice was a perfect prescription for me, and it got me through many hopeless days. But I still wept often. The pain went so deep that it made me angry with God and tired of the pay-to-prosper message to which I had become accustomed.

You see, I was not only a church "tither"; I was a "*more-than-*tither." I gave offerings, seed offerings, special offerings, missions offerings, alms, first-fruits, and building pledges. I participated in nearly every pseudo-biblical offering taken. Yet I still did not receive the "breakthrough" which was guaranteed to sacrificial tithers. I became upset with God. "I have given sacrificially in every possible way, so how could He allow me to go through such financial pain?" I demanded. I felt like I had a good reason to be upset, since I made sacrifices beyond reason. For example, have you ever pushed your car home from church? I have.

One night, while volunteering for a Christian concert, I was asked to make a supply-run to the store. Understanding that I was almost out of gasoline and had little money for more (I was a full-time student, while interning part-time without pay) my supervisor assured me that I would be provided with money for fuel upon my return. So I went on the supply run, and *saved the day*. Upon my return, however, the supervisor went back on our deal; I was given no gas money. Just before midnight I had finally finished my post-volunteering clean-up duties, then my wife and I got in our car, and (since we were doing the Lord's work) prayed to God that we would make it home on our meager supply of fuel. One-half mile later the car sputtered to a stop. It was out of gas. I had to get out and *push my car* up the road toward home. According to the prosperity message I should have been pushing home *wheelbarrows full of money*, not a car empty of gas! I don't know how many church-folk leaving the concert passed me that night, but it was a kind police officer who stopped to help me push. And as my beautiful wife wept in our 230,000-mile automobile, I realized that the "prosperity message" does not work. Our only hope was for our condo to sell. If it did not, we would surely find ourselves financially *shipwrecked*.

The difference between life's storms and life's shipwrecks is a significant one. In a typical storm (even a financial one) if you can wait it out for long enough, then everything will be alright. The storm must pass sometime. Sooner or later you will get another job and be able to pay your overdue bills. However, sometimes the storm is so massive that the only way out is to run your ship aground. These are *life's shipwrecks*. At these rare times, it is certain you will not escape without accruing major damage and long-term consequences. This damage might come in the form of a home foreclosure, a bankruptcy, or sadly even a divorce. You will survive, but you will also have much to rebuild afterwards. In a shipwreck, life takes-on added dimensions of difficulty.

However, if you are a shipwreck victim don't think that life is over for you. Far from it! The Apostle Paul was forced into a shipwreck, also. Yet, Paul's distressing experience only opened another door which allowed him to accomplish even more than he anticipated. Your shipwreck will do the same for you. There are opportunities which await victims of life's shipwrecks that other travelers will never have. This becomes clear as Paul's storm continues.

Paul had been pleading God to preserve the lives of his 275 shipmates, and an angel informed Paul that his request had been granted. This must have brought great relief to the crew as Paul relayed the message. However they likely recoiled as Paul told them about the catch: "However, we must run aground on a certain island" (Acts 27:26, NKJV). The text continues:

> Now when the fourteenth night had come, as we were driven up and down in the Adriatic *Sea,* about midnight the sailors sensed they were drawing near some land. And they took soundings and found *it* to be twenty fathoms; and when they had gone a little farther, they took soundings again and found *it* to be fifteen fathoms. Then, fearing lest we should run aground on the rocks, they dropped four anchors from the stern, and prayed for day to come. And as the sailors were seeking to escape from the ship, when they had let down the skiff into the sea, under pretense of putting out anchors from the prow, Paul said to the centurion and the soldiers, "Unless these men stay in the ship, you cannot be saved." Then the soldiers cut away the ropes of the skiff and let it fall off (Acts 27:27–32, NKJV).

Probably none of the sailors were hoping to end their journey by smashing the ship to pieces on the rocks of an unknown island. After all, shipwrecks are not known for being kind to those involved. Even if they were to live through it, nobody could predict what dangerous surprises awaited them on that island, or even *if* they would ever be rescued *from* it. Certainly they would have been thankful for Paul's hope of survival, but there were probably too many question marks for the group to feel totally comfortable with a shipwreck. In fact, the professional sailors were so uncomfortable with this plan that they tried to jump-ship so they could safely *row* ashore, leaving the rest to perish (Acts 27:30). They were clearly not in favor of the shipwreck arrangement.

You might also be approaching your own shipwreck. Your job is in jeopardy or was already terminated, your bills are past-due, and your credit cards are all maxed-out. Your back is already against the wall and if one more setback happens, your life will be seriously ruined, you calculate. When you think life couldn't get any worse and you have exhausted every possible option to avert disaster but nothing changes, then you are facing one of life's *shipwrecks*. If this describes you, then I must warn you that soon you will be faced with a decision. You will either choose to follow the example of the professional mariners, or you will choose to follow Paul's lead. There is no third option.

As humans, when our back is against the wall, fear kicks-in and we automatically go into the "fight or flight" mode. "How can I preserve myself (my job, my finances, my image, etc.) in this situation?" we instinctively calculate. The only answer we will accept is the one which leaves us in our best possible situation, even if it costs the lives or careers of family, friends, coworkers, or who-knows-what-else. Our instincts act to preserve *ourselves*, regardless of anybody else, and even at the cost of *everybody else*. This is why the professional sailors reacted as they did. They knew that shipwrecks often kill all aboard, and they understood that their best chance to see another day was to row ashore in the small boat which could only carry a few people. These "goons" were not about to go down with their ship, yet in their escape attempt they knowing gave everyone else a death-sentence.

Both Paul and these crewmembers were needed to get the ship's passengers to safety. Paul had the insight to direct the ship where to go, and the sailors had the necessary knowledge and skill to get it there. *Both* were necessary for everybody's well-being in this situation. However, while the crew attempted to use their abilities to benefit *only themselves* (at the expense of all), Paul used his abilities to benefit *everybody*.

You see, Paul knew what the sailors were doing and he could have easily "cut a deal" to secure a seat in the skiff. But he didn't. Instead, Paul took the high road. In essence, the professional sailors were motivated by fear of the situation, which enacted their self-preservation mechanisms, while Paul was motivated by God's peace and love for others. *Only God's love can motivate somebody to give of themselves for the good of others.* Paul intimately knew God's love, which was how he could find the will and strength to help everybody, instead of only himself.

When the ship is about to sink, each person's actions reveal their true motives. They will either help *others*, or help *only themselves* at other's expense. This is the true measure of a man or woman. It doesn't take greatness or courage to shove others out of the way (and into certain death) to find one's own escape—this is what cowards do. But it takes tremendous courage to *do what is right* even when one's life is on the line, and there seems to be no benefit for right-doing. A good person will do what is right when they see a benefit; a *great* person will do what is right even when they see no benefit at all. Yet, there is *always* a benefit to doing what is right. The benefit may not be immediately available or readily apparent, nonetheless it *does* exist. *God rewards right-doing.* He always has and He always will. Psalm 145 declares, "The LORD preserves all who love Him, but all the wicked He will destroy" (Psalm 145:20, NKJV). The reward for right-doing may be instantaneous, or it may be awaiting the individual's grand entrance into heaven (see 1 Peter 1:11), but either way there is *always* a reward for doing right.

As your own shipwreck approaches, your adrenaline will begin pumping as you enter your self-preservation mode. You will discover new ways to save yourself at other's expense. During company cutbacks you will be tempted to denigrate your coworkers to preserve your own job. After all, if you can pin a target on somebody else's back you might keep one off of your own. During financial recessions you might be tempted to lie to credit lenders, cheat on your taxes, shoplift from the store, or steal from your neighbor. Measures which before you would have never considered will suddenly become realistic options. In my own life I have even recently considered spending my last two dollars (literally) on a couple of scratch-off lottery tickets! (I have caught myself attempting to rationalize this absurd behavior by thinking it might be God's way of providing me with some gas-money.)

The truth is, the world is brimming with people who sacrifice their own chance to "be great" for a fleeting gain at others' expense. They would rather do what they *know to be wrong*, and thereby become a *goon*, than do what they *know to be right* and become a *great*. Don't *you* make this same mistake as the professional sailors in our story; instead, follow Paul's lead. Don't let fear enter your heart, and *don't do anything* while your adrenaline is pumping. Instead, spend time in God's presence and remain in His calming peace. Be certain that *all* of your actions would make God proud of your decisions. Find ways to do what is right and good even when it hurts, and even though you cannot see any benefit at all. God will love you for it (John 14:21). Any *goon* can take advantage of the vulnerable, and shove them out of the way to forge an escape path. But it takes a *great* person to pick-up the helpless and carry them out of the fire with you. One day soon, when your unavoidable shipwreck becomes unbearably close, you will be faced with this choice. At that moment, and by your actions, you will either choose to be a *goon*, or you will choose to be a *great*. Please choose wisely.

Another significant aspect to notice is, while the sailors attempted to help themselves at others' expense, Paul helped himself *by* helping others. The principle is this: *if you will help others, you will also have helped yourself.* Most people ignore this alternative and only help themselves at the expense of others. They have not learned that *they* would *also* benefit, if they would only do what is right and help others.

Carl is in the construction business. Because of the housing market slump in his area, he has had difficulty finding work. Meanwhile, he heard that one of his Christian friends in town was having trouble renting their second home because of its poor condition. Always eager to help a friend, Carl offered an arrangement: he would renovate the home free-of-charge in exchange for the renting it upon completion. The friend accepted, thankful to have hope for his dilapidated rental, and the two shook hands. Two months later the project was nearly complete, and the house looked *great*. At that point, the friend reneged on the deal and booted Carl from the premises. No payment. No place to live. Not even a note of thanks. And since they had agreed with only a simple handshake, there was nothing Carl could do about it.

This "friend" threw Carl under the bus, instead of helping him in return. The opportunity for both parties to benefit was there, but because of self-serving actions, it was forever lost. It would have been to the friend's advantage if he had simply done what is right in the situation and fulfilled his part of the agreement, or even chosen to pay Carl for his work. Instead he opted for wrongdoing and a broken friendship. This friend became a *goon*, and in doing so, he sacrificed his chance to be a *great*. Needless to say, this hurt Carl tremendously, and sadly, both parties lost-out.

On the other side of the coin, I have witnessed people in severe hardships find ways to give to others in need. This benefits both parties, as the receiver abounds with hope and thanksgiving, and the giver receives unspeakable joy from God. Amazing! The receiver receives material blessings, and the giver receives spiritual blessings. This is a practical demonstration of a living faith empowered by God's love (see 2 Corinthians 9:12–15). It is a win-win situation.

When you do what is right in your situation, you just might be surprised at the benefits. If you will help your struggling coworkers, then your boss might realize that you are a company-strengthening asset and will decide she *can't afford* to let you go! Or maybe you will still get canned, only to learn that one of your company's clients has noticed your honesty and dedication, and hires you the very next day for a higher salary—this actually happened to a friend of mine! The possibilities are endless, yet the benefits remain certain for those who will just have the courage to *do the right thing.*

> And as day was about to dawn, Paul implored *them* all to take food, saying, "Today is the fourteenth day you have waited and continued without food, and eaten nothing. Therefore I urge you to take nourishment, for this is for your survival, since not a hair will fall from the head of any of you." And when he had said these things, he took bread and gave thanks to God in the presence of them all; and when he had broken *it* he began to eat. Then they were all encouraged, and also took food themselves. And in all we were two hundred and seventy-six persons on the ship. So when they had eaten enough, they lightened the ship and threw out the wheat into the sea (Acts 27:33–38, NKJV).

I want to challenge you to look at Paul's position through this situation. He was not *one iota* better-off than anybody else around him. He was in the same *ship*, the same *sea*, and the same *storm* as everybody else. He was just as hungry, and thirsty, and probably just as sea-sick as the rest of those onboard, also. Ultimately Paul's fate was no different than anybody else's fate. But there was one major difference between the rest of the crew and Paul: *Paul had hope from God*, while the others did not.

Our principle for application is this: *you don't need to be out of your own pit before you can give hope to others.* In order to be an instrument of hope, you only need to be firmly connected to the Giver of hope, which is God. It is easy to assume that we can't really help anybody else, until we get out of our own junk. We presume that since we are in the same boat as others, that they wouldn't believe that we have the answer to life's problems. However, Paul was in the same horrible circumstances as his shipmates, yet he held *the ultimate answer* to their problems. This allowed him to distribute his hope to those who were in his boat, while still in the storm. You see, *hope is not found in circumstances going well.* If it was, then Paul would have been just as hopeless as the rest. Yet Paul had enough hope to spare, simply because he *remained connected to God.*

Paul's story challenges each of us to be instruments of hope to others *while you are still in your difficulties,* not afterwards. *Afterwards* does not benefit those in the disaster with you. They don't need hope *later*; they need it *now.* Take some time and listen to the precious folks in *your* boat, and you will realize the size of their problems. Their marriages are falling apart, their children are dealing drugs and involved in prostitution, and they just found a cancerous lump. When you hear their stories, you will realize that your own problems pale in comparison. The amazing thing is this: if you know Jesus Christ as your personal Lord and Savior, then *you have what they need.* You have a God with the answers to *all* of their problems, and He will give them hope to boot!

You see, hope is never based upon circumstances, such as a job, an income, or even a nest egg. Money can provide a level of security, but it *cannot* give hope. Security of any means is no more than a *defensive* mechanism intended to thwart possible negative circumstances. Meanwhile hope is an *offensive* mechanism guaranteed to ensure future positive circumstances. Even at its best, security can only protect you from things getting *worse.* But in contrast, hope always guarantees that things will get *better.* Further, hope comes from having God, not money. Hope comes from simply believing that God is a good Father, and that good fathers take good care of their children. And it doesn't cost *a dime* to believe this.

There is no charge to believe God and receive this hope. Yet once you have hope you can distribute it generously. When others see your genuine optimistic anticipation in the midst of their same circumstances, then they will become hopeful and encouraged also. They will ask how you can still smile when life stinks; and you will have a good answer for them. These folks need hope while they are in their difficulties, otherwise some of them won't make it *through* their struggles. God used Paul to bring hope to others in his same predicament, and He wants to do the same with *you*.

The last time Paul volunteered information it was rejected, but this time his advice was valued. Everybody followed Paul's example in eating one last meal before they tossed the remaining food overboard. Most surprising is the fact that Paul "gave thanks" to God with everybody else in attendance. This is incredible! All of the sailors, soldiers, and passengers bowed their heads and thanked Paul's God for His promise to them, and *joy abounded* throughout the meal.

I believe this indicates that at least some, and possibly even all, of Paul's shipmates received spiritual salvation that day. Maybe they embraced Christianity at that moment, or possibly later professed it based upon this event. We may never know the exact results, but we do know that God touched the hearts of 275 frightened people that day, and it rocked them to their core. And it all happened because God cared enough to put a Christian in the sinking ship with them.

Still, Paul's problems did not instantly vanish when his shipmates bowed their heads in prayer, however. If God's purpose with the storm was limited to Paul reaching his 275 sojourners, then we would expect the storm to have subsided immediately. After all, *that* would be a miracle! Instead, however, the storm continued to rage. This is an indication that Paul's work on this voyage was not yet complete. There was still more to do. The crew was forced to raise the sail again and run the vessel onto the coastal rocks of an unknown island.

To be shipwrecked sounds dangerous and frightening. But to be shipwrecked on a *certain island* (Acts 27:26) sounds precise, even deliberate. To be sure, it was both. You see, this storm was not nature's chaotic episode; it was God's *calculated plan*. From the outset of their journey *God orchestrated their shipwreck*.

During the storm, the crew could see neither sun, nor moon, nor stars, making them absolutely clueless as to their location. So God Himself stepped-in as the ship's Captain. For fourteen days He maneuvered the vessel by steering each isolated wave, guiding every current, and directing each solitary gust of wind to bring the ship over 500 miles, to ensure they arrived at a specific island called Malta. Isn't this amazing? When the human captain could no longer man the helm, God literally took control and harnessed billions of individual forces to usher the ship's precious crew and passengers to a place of safety. And from the maps in the back of your Bible, you'll notice that there weren't a whole lot of places where safety was even possible.

You might feel like you are at the mercy of your storm, just like Paul's ship was. Without a guiding light, you could be unsure of where you are at in life, and also uncertain of your future. But *you are still on God's radar*. He knows where you are, *and* He knows right where to bring you. If God harnessed all the forces of nature to usher Paul to his appointed destination, then He will harness all the forces of life to deliver *you* to your destiny, also. Even though you don't exactly understand how the forces of difficulties and circumstances affect your life and future, God does. He has been orchestrating everything in your storm to bring you to *a certain place in life*.

You probably never intended to go to this new place in life. Paul hadn't. He was simply trying to get to Rome. He never hoped to wreck his ship on an unknown island. If Paul had his way, he would have avoided the mess altogether, but there were decisions made which were beyond his control. Likewise, nobody today aspires to ruin their finances with a shameful bankruptcy, or crash their marriage with divorce. Just like with Paul, often these things happen because of actions and circumstances beyond our control. We can no more control the national economy or ensure a spouse's fidelity than Paul could control the decisions of his Roman Centurion guard. Sometimes these things happen even when nobody intended for them to happen. And when they do, life becomes messy. Yet, although God did not cause your mess, He has a plan for you *through* it.

The point is this: s*torms in life can be God's method of diverting you to your own "Malta."* Your Malta might be a time to earn your college degree, or to get a different job at another company. It could be a completely new career path, or even a successful marriage. But one thing is for sure: *God plans to bless you and make you a blessing there.* In Acts chapter 28 we find that Paul's Malta was a safe-haven for him and the crew. If you need a safe-haven from today's difficulties and problems, then your Malta is the key. At Paul's Malta, there were people willing to help him with his physical needs of warmth and protection. These kind people await you at *your*

Malta, too. After your long and arduous journey, you will be pleasantly surprised at the blessings you receive at your Malta. Paul was.

For Paul, this shipwreck was also an opportunity to do the Lord's work. He had been faithful to reach-out to his 275, and now God had given him a bigger stage to reach more people. Paul was not being *punished* by his shipwreck . . . he was being *promoted* by it. This is seen in that Paul was God's chosen servant who effectively reached Malta's inhabitants with the power of God. In his three months there, Paul healed many people of various diseases, including the father of the island's chief Roman official, Publius. Through this healing ministry, much of the island recognized the greatness of Jesus Christ, and I'm sure that some received spiritual salvation. It is important to understand that reaching Malta was not Paul's life-purpose . . . it was *a bonus*. Instead of dying in a shipwreck, Paul reached an entire island because of it! Talk about an effective detour!

Similarly, your Malta will be a place where you can minister to others, just as Paul did. Your Malta is your promotion to reach more people, and these people won't care about your shipwreck. They won't mind your spotted background, or your checkered history; they will simply be pleased with what you have to offer. And don't think you have to be an overt evangelist or have a nation-wide healing ministry, either. *Whatever it is* that you have to offer is *exactly* what they need. This is why God arranged to bring you there.

> When it was day, they did not recognize the land; but they observed a bay with a beach, onto which they planned to run the ship if possible. And they let go the anchors and left *them* in the sea, meanwhile loosing the rudder ropes; and they hoisted the mainsail to the wind and made for shore. But striking a place where two seas met, they ran the ship aground; and the prow stuck fast and remained immovable, but the stern was being broken up by the violence of the waves. And the soldiers' plan was to kill the prisoners, lest any of them should swim away and escape. But the centurion, wanting to save Paul, kept them from *their* purpose, and commanded that those who could swim should jump *overboard* first and get to land, and the rest, some on boards and some on *parts* of the ship. And so it was that they all escaped safely to land (Acts 27:39–44, NKJV).

I love the beginning of this passage: "When it was day" (Acts 27:39, NKJV). Even after the darkest and longest night, the day always follows.

This will be true for you, also. No matter how long your storm has been, *daylight is on its way*! In God's creation, night cannot last forever. The brightness of day must eventually prevail. Life will get better, because it *must* get better.

This brings me back to my condominium story. After ten long months of unsuccessfully trying to sell the condo unit, I had given-up all hope. Exhausted, I was resigned to whatever fate awaited me and my credit. Hope was gone. Even the real estate agent had all but given-up, and allowed our contract to expire. Nothing could be done. My dream of being a minister was completely destroyed because of my inevitable foreclosure. Then, just days before the bank initiated the foreclosure I received a call from the realtor. There was an interested party, and the realtor needed to renew our contract so he could negotiate the sale. Shortly thereafter the paperwork was finalized; the condo was sold. My perfect storm was *over*.

Maybe your storm has not yet subsided. Possibly you are still headed toward complete personal ruin. Or maybe you have already experienced a major shipwreck in life, yet your storm continues to rage. Remember, *just because your storm is not over does not mean that your life is*. You are not a bad Christian, and God has not written-off, or abandoned you. To the contrary, He has been working to reach others *through you* during your storm. When your work is complete, your storm will end. Until then, there remains more for you to do. With this in mind, keep yourself in peace by spending time with God every day. Help others through this storm, instead of sacrificing them for your own good. Continue to do what is right, even if it hurts. Persist in reaching-out to those around you—they *need* you right now.

God knows the work is hard. He really does. It was difficult for Paul, also. But continue being faithful, and when the work is over there will be a time for you to rest. Day always follows even the darkest night. During your storm God has been dutifully carrying you to your own place of rest and relaxation—your own *Malta*. After all, you have *earned* the R&R. There the people will welcome you with open arms, they will show you great kindness, but they won't care about your past. When you arrive you will find that your shipwreck is nothing more than a distant and foggy memory, and once again, life will be *good*. And doesn't that sound *nice*?

Discussion Questions

1. What is the difference between a storm of life, and a shipwreck of life? Do you feel as though you are in either of these? Why?

2. "What should I do?" is a question which every shipwreck victim asks themselves before their actual crash. What are the only two options one can choose when put in this situation, and what is the difference between them?

3. Which of these two options do you think God wants you to choose? Why? What are some practical steps you can take to ensure that you act/react to your shipwreck in a God-honoring way?

4. Is there always a reward/benefit for doing what is right? Why or why not?

5. Is it possible to help others, and in doing so, to help yourself? Why or why not?

6. Have you witnessed instances in which someone used their circumstances to be great, or to be a "goon"? How so?

7. What do you need to be able to rise above your circumstances and help others?

8. Is hope found in circumstances going well? Why or why not?

9. When is the appropriate time to be instruments of hope to those around us: after our difficulties or during them?

10. Can you think of ways in which God has been orchestrating your shipwreck? Why or why not? (Remember, sometimes we can't foresee our safe landing until after it happens.)

11. At this time, can you imagine what your own "Malta" might look like?

5

But I Don't Want to Move

Joseph and Mary: God's Witness Relocation Program

(LUKE 2:1–7, MATTHEW 2:1–11)

*Difficulties are God's errands; and when we are sent upon them
we should esteem it a proof of God's confidence
—as a compliment from God.*

—HENRY WARD BEECHER

WITH EACH TRIP TO the store my son expands his Christmas wish
list. An impetuous and expressive five-year old, he explores the
eye-level toys and products, then explains in creative detail why it is
imperative that he receives each one. He wants motion picture actions
figures, super-hero costumes, toy swords, spaceships, video games, and
most everything else found in the toy aisles. As his father, I have learned
to listen, but not act. It has taken some practice, but I can now gauge
which items he *really* wants by the frequency of his request. If, after
the trip to the store, he never again mentions the toy, then I dismiss it.
However, if he continues to prod me toward the particular item days
after our shopping trip, I take note that he is serious about the toy. You
see, I want to give him truly meaningful gifts, instead of fleeting fancies.
Sometimes he gets what he asked for, and sometimes he gets something
completely different. Like any parent, I hope to exceed his expectations
(without breaking my budget, that is).

Before the first Christmas the people of Israel also had a wish-list,
and *deliverance* was at the top. They had been asking God to deliver

them from Roman tyranny and military occupation of their homeland. They wanted a chance to live free from the corruption of pagan people and practices. These appeared to be big-ticket items, but they were small compared to what Israel really needed. In fact, what Israel needed was also needed by the entire world, and God was planning it for that very first Christmas.

> And it came to pass in those days *that* a decree went out from Caesar Augustus that all the world should be registered. This census first took place while Quirinius was governing Syria. So all went to be registered, everyone to his own city. Joseph also went up from Galilee, out of the city of Nazareth, into Judea, to the city of David, which is called Bethlehem, because he was of the house and lineage of David, to be registered with Mary, his betrothed wife, who was with child. So it was, that while they were there, the days were completed for her to be delivered. And she brought forth her firstborn Son, and wrapped Him in swaddling cloths, and laid Him in a manger, because there was no room for them in the inn (Luke 2:1–7, NKJV).

Caesar's decree was not a popular one, as it probably forced many people into discomfort or even hardship. Today's economy has done the same, creating a frightening tension which has gripped the entire world. But I don't need to tell you, because you likely have this fear of the future already lodged in your heart. There is nothing more alarming than an unknown future. If you have lost your job, then you fear the consequences of being unable to pay for your housing. If your pay has been significantly reduced, you are likely to be worried about how to still put food on the table. Or, maybe your concern is whether your current employment will even last for another week.

Through the midst of this storm of uncertainty, many are making important life decisions based on necessity, instead of desire. People are changing careers, not because the new one pays more, but because the old one ended early. Scores of folks are moving across the country, not because a pay raise awaits their arrival, but because they were laid off last month and heard there is work out west (or, east). Even further, extended families are living under the same roof, not to strengthen family bonds, but to simply survive the recession. In short, whereas people used to make changes based upon *positive motivations*, now *negative cir-*

cumstances dictate their course of life. As Christians living in America, we are not used to God leading us in this way.

Most of us have become accustomed to God using *positive motivation* to encourage us to make major transitions in life. We have been taught to ask God for His Kingdom to come by way of higher pay and lower taxes, and we expect Him to lead us through life by forging a broad path of favorable circumstances. During times of transition we often "discern" God's will, not by prayer, but by crunching the financial numbers. We don't feel bad about uprooting our families and moving across the country if it will afford a higher income and a bigger house, regardless of any spiritual dimension. In fact, you have probably heard other Christians declare, "I'll know God wants me to move to [insert city/state here] because I'll get a promotion or pay-raise to go." In the boom of American prosperity this often worked, too! But times have changed.

These days it is common for *negative pressures* to strip-away our resources and options, and thereby force us to move (or to move-in with family) just to get by. And we wonder why God has allowed it. Our predictable God has become unpredictable, and this makes us uneasy. Although it may be uncomfortable to accept, Joseph and Mary's story demonstrates that God *can* and sometimes *does* lead His children using both positive incentives *and* negative pressures.

I worked at a minimum-wage part-time position when the economy forced my employer to downsize. Six of us lower-tier workers lost our only job, and we were all faced with the harsh reality that without a job our family would have no home and no food. Forced to react, most of us had only one remaining solution to our immediate problem: move-in with the relatives. Of six unemployed workers, five of us began living with extended family, while only one moved out of state to take another position. Clearly, the rules have changed for Christians in America. This is exactly why so many people have recently become uncertain of God's leading. Today's economic chaos has thrown many God-fearing believers into a tailspin. Many of us erroneously assume we have offended God, and we don't even know how!

Mary and Joseph might also have thought they did something wrong. As they faced an unwed pregnancy, an arduous journey, and a baby born in a cow shed (a less romanticized description of a manger), they might have wondered where they veered from God's path. At some point they might have begun to wonder if God had abandoned them. As if their own self-accusations weren't enough, there were probably others who would have been happy to accuse the couple of wrongdoing. You have probably noticed that most people don't mind imposing their dogmatic beliefs into other's lives. However, God had not *abandoned* Mary and Joseph to their circumstances; to the contrary God was *arranging* their circumstances in order to bless them tremendously. Their part was only to *be patient* through their ordeal.

It is important to note that the governmental mandate was the only known reason for Mary and Joseph's move to Bethlehem. Nowhere in Scripture do we find Mary campaigning for a warmer southern home to better endure the winter months, or Joseph considering moving to where carpenters were paid top-shekel. Their only earthly reason for moving was because a governmental mandate *forced* them to go. To be sure, God needed Mary in Bethlehem to fulfill the prophecy of the Savior's birthplace. But He used Caesar's mandate to make it happen.

At this point I want you to note that God could have simply *asked* the couple to go to Bethlehem, but He did not. He allowed them to be pushed around by a heavy-handed government, and He did not intervene. This particular insight carries such weight because it is at the crux of today's dilemma for many American Christians. Most of us have been taught that God is nice and always works in nice ways. We have been led to believe that God will angel-deliver an invitation if He wants us to go to Milwaukee (or any other place), and then we expect Him to confirm it with Scripture. *Then*, if we are *still* not convinced, we are supposed to "lay-out a fleece" (like Gideon did in Judges 6:36–40) and wait for God to answer with a *sign from heaven*. But the truth is, sometimes the only sign we get is the "For Sale" sign the bank plants in our front yard.

The point is this: God doesn't work according to an "American church-approved" program. In fact, He doesn't conform to *any* program. Even further, God doesn't want His people to follow a program, either. Instead, He wants us to follow a *Person*—Jesus Christ. You see, anybody can memorize religious slogans and practice religious duties without personally knowing God. However, as Christians, our religious duty is to *know God* and to *make Him known* (see Ephesians 3:10, and 2 Corinthians 5:20). This absolutely cannot be done by merely utilizing a program, regardless of how good the program is. God wants us to know *Him*, and to follow and trust Him even when we don't understand what is going on in our lives—*especially* when we don't understand what is going on in our lives.

So don't expect a flowery path of roses to carry you through your transitions in life, because God probably won't give it to you. Instead, learn a lesson from Mary and Joseph: *roll with the punches*. During tough times, set aside what you *want* to do in life, and do what you *must* do to get by. When you can't find a job in your current field, look in another. When the bank kicks you out of your house, stay with relatives or friends. And when life doesn't work-out for you in one town, move to another. The chances are God has already informed you where He wants you to go. And if you are resisting, then please realize that God knows how to "put the kibosh" on your opposing efforts. Jonah finally caught onto this concept when he was in the belly of the fish (see Jonah chapters 1–3)—*please* don't make God do a repeat. If your "ideal" life has just been un-idealized, don't go to drinking, drugs, or depression . . . just go to Milwaukee.

This brings us to another point: *God uses all circumstances in the lives of His children to ensure that His purpose is ultimately accomplished.* External realities like the economy, government, and your employment situation are not outside of God's plan. God actually uses them to accomplish His will. Unknowingly and unintentionally, each of these entities plays right into God's hand. For example, the census edict came from none other than Caesar Augustus, the ruler of the entire Roman Empire. The Book of Proverbs says, "The king's heart *is* in the hand of the LORD, *like* the rivers of water; He turns it wherever He wishes" (Proverbs 21:1, NKJV). God *can*, and *will*, change the heart of any king or president or CEO, to accomplish the heavenly plan.

In this case, God stirred the heart of Caesar August, and in effect, *moved the entire Roman Empire,* just to deliver Mary and Joseph to Bethlehem, so they could fulfill their destiny! God will move the hearts of the most powerful people on earth, as if they were pawns in His chess-game, just to get you to your next step in life. *Nobody* can stand in the way of you completing your destiny, and any ruler who tries will only become frustrated as they find themselves actually *helping* your efforts.

Likewise, your *difficulties of today* are actually *helping* you to accomplish your *destiny of tomorrow.* A troubled economy cannot hinder you from fulfilling your God-given mandate. Neither can an empty bank account, or even the loss of your job. Regardless of what your situation is, *absolutely nothing* can hinder you from fulfilling your destiny. You probably don't appreciate today's troubled economy or your position in it, but it is exactly the impetus you need to get you where God is bringing you.

Although Caesar Augustus gave the census edict, the Jewish King Herod enforced it in his territories. Moreover, it is possible that King Herod even used this census to try to *find* and *kill* the Baby Jesus. From Joseph and Mary's perspective, had they known Herod's evil intentions they might have gone straight to Egypt, and totally missed fulfilling the greatest prophecy of all-time! As a good father-figure, Joseph would have likely averted Bethlehem to protect his family, if he would have known Herod's scheme. Any reasonable person would have done the same. However, had they bypassed their Bethlehem appointment, the fulfillment of the most important Scriptural prophecy of all-time would have been thrown into jeopardy!

Christ's birthplace was such an important cornerstone of messianic prophecy that even if all other elements of Jesus' life remained *exactly the same*, with the single exception of Him being born somewhere other than Bethlehem, God's plan for the redemption of mankind would be *forever lost*. In other words, *there was no "plan B"*; the baby *must* be born in Bethlehem. As fantastic as it may sound, the success of mankind's redemption from sin was dependent upon Mary and Joseph's uncomfortable transition. Maybe the success of *your* future depends upon your transition, also. You may want to abandon the effort, but that that would only keep you from fulfilling your destiny. The end purpose will be exciting, but the path leading there will not be what you anticipated. It will have unexpected turns and uncomfortable transitions.

You might have to move across country, like I did. Or you may have to move-in with your in-laws for a season. I did this, too. However, this is (arguably) better than moving-in with the animals like Mary and Joseph's situation required! After graduation from seminary I had no other option but to continue at my minimum-wage part-time job, and therefore did not make enough money to rent an apartment for my family. Thankfully, my wife's parents lived nearby and graciously allowed us to stay with them for a time.

Although this was not my hoped-for arrangement, I was thankful to have a roof over my family's heads. We shared space by living three people to a room, and we shared bills to make the money go further. These circumstances felt cramped, but we were determined to make the best of our situation together, even though it wasn't easy.

After several months I began to discover that there really are blessings to living with in-laws. My wife's parents saw the birth of our daughter, and our children grew to love their grandparents. While I worked, my wife enjoyed her parent's company, and their help with our newborn. My wife and I developed a closer bond with our children than existed when we enjoyed more spacious accommodations. And I found myself better understanding my in-laws, and became more appreciative of them. However, our trials didn't end there. Before my family made it to our own "Malta" we lived with *six other families* (mostly relatives) for short periods of time. With each stay we found ourselves blessed in many ways, and I believe our hosts would say the same, as we sought to be a blessing in return. The Old Testament character Ruth modeled this concept of being a blessing to her in-law relatives (Ruth 1:14–18, 22); maybe God wants *you* to follow suit.

Or possibly you won't have to move-in with your in-laws; instead *they* might be forced to move-in with *you!* Sometimes God expects our hospitality for family or friends in need. It is telling that in all Joseph's own *hometown* he could find nowhere to stay; don't let this be the testimony of *your* family. Sadly, nobody in Bethlehem nobody offered their spare room to the hometown boy and his nine-month pregnant wife. In 2000 years society has not changed much in this respect.

Don't be surprised if no one in your network of family and friends is willing to help you either. It happened to Joseph, and if you are following God's path, then it might happen to you, too. Moreover, don't expect wealthy church members to come to your rescue; they did not get rich by giving-away their money, and they probably aren't going to start now. James was much harsher in his condemnation of rich church-members: "Indeed the wages of the laborers who mowed your fields, which you kept back by fraud cry out; and the cries of the reapers have reached the ears of the Lord of Sabaoth [the armies]" (James 5:4, NKJV). Instead, any help you need will come from those who can hardly afford to do so. These folks barely scrape-by from week to week, but somehow they always manage to give something to someone else in need. These special people know what it is like to suffer hardship, so they go out of their way to help alleviate the burden of others. A lesson from this first Christmas story is: *help often comes in unexpected ways and from unexpected sources.* Joseph and Mary didn't expect an animal-shed, but they were glad for this small help when nothing else became available.

Through it all, your difficult transition will provide you with many blessings which you haven't even considered, just like my in-law arrangement. Maybe your greatest assignment right now is to not only learn how to get-along with your in-laws, but to learn to appreciate them and be a blessing to them. That was my assignment from God for about a year. Or possibly your mission is to strengthen your family-unit so God can accomplish your *big-ticket prayer request* without your home-life falling apart. Or possibly humility is your greatest need, which is why God keeps putting you in situations which you have no control over. You may not understand the *reason* for your immediate discomfort; nevertheless, there *is* one. And in the end you will be better off for having gone through it. In short, *your troubles are for your own good*, and so are mine.

In the Christmas story there were a million things which could have gone wrong to ruin God's plan. To name a few, Mary could have disbelieved or refused the angel's message. Joseph could have divorced Mary because of her unexpected pregnancy. Caesar could have *not* given the edict forcing everyone to their hometowns. Mary might have miscarried the baby from the difficult journey to Bethlehem. The couple could have been assaulted on their journey by roadway thieves. Mary might have given birth *before arriving* in Bethlehem. Herod's men could have identified the couple and killed the baby. The wise men could have returned to inform Herod of the precise location of baby-Jesus. Etc, etc, etc—you get the point. But God ensured the proper outcome of *every one* of these possibilities, and even more.

Likewise, there are a million things which could go awry and completely ruin your life and destiny . . . *but God won't let that happen.* The Lord was attentive to every detail of Mary and Joseph's plight, and He is no less attentive to yours today. He will take care of every detail of your life, protecting you at every corner, and providing for you at every crossroads to ensure His ultimate plan for you is accomplished.

Your life is important; the Bible does not guarantee that another person will be able to reach the individuals who *you* are destined to reach. You see, your destiny is *your destiny*. No one else can fulfill it. If you aren't able to fulfill it, then many precious folks who you are destined to reach may never have another chance to hear the life-changing message of Jesus Christ. For many of these people there is no "plan-B"; *you* are their only answer.

> Now there were in the same country shepherds living out in the fields, keeping watch over their flock by night. And, behold, an angel of the Lord stood before them, and the glory of the Lord

shone around them, and they were greatly afraid. Then the angel said to them, "Do not be afraid, for behold, I bring you good tidings of great joy which will be to all people. For there is born to you this day in the city of David a Savior, who is Christ the Lord. And this *will be* the sign to you: You will find a Babe wrapped in swaddling cloths, lying in a manger." And suddenly there was with the angel a multitude of the heavenly host praising God and saying: "Glory to God in the highest, And on earth peace, goodwill toward men!" (Luke 2:8–14, NKJV).

Have you ever wondered the reason for the Son of God to enter this world under such dire conditions? I believe God did this to demonstrate that He is willing to connect with mankind even at the "lowest" level. Even the poorest, most miserable living condition imaginable is not able to devalue a human life. I believe this was God's way of demonstrating that He cares for those who the rest of the world despises. So, even if you are so destitute that you live in a cardboard home, please know that your life is of inestimable value, because you are made in God's image. Nothing can take-away this tremendous status. In fact, according to Jesus, you have got more going for you than the haughty rich folks who snub their noses at you: "Blessed *are you* poor, for yours is the kingdom of God" (Luke 6:20, NKJV). You may not have much on earth, but you have God's kingdom.

In early 2009 a British man had a heart attack in his home. According to the news report, he managed to call the emergency hotline, and inform the dispatcher of his crisis before he drifted unconscious.[3] The man and the telephone both fell to the floor. Two paramedics arrived at the doorway to find the man lying unconscious and near death on the floor. However, they took the time to also notice the man's living conditions, noting that his home was *extremely* messy. This sickening discovery dissuaded the paramedics from entering, and even initiated their discussion as to whether the man was even worth saving. Withholding assistance, the pair discussed their plan to falsely report that they found the man dead upon their arrival. The victim's last few breaths slipped away as the pair devised their scheme. The only thing they did not calculate into their alibi was the fact that the telephone dispatcher was still on the line, and *heard every word they said.*

To these two paramedic's, the worth of a human life was based upon a standard of cleanliness. If this were the case with God, He would have never allowed His own Son to born in an animal-shed. I believe God's

Son was born in a manger because He wanted to emphasize the fact that *every* human life, even those found in the worst of all conditions, is still of immeasurable value. When Jesus walked the earth He was a friend of lepers, healing these untouchables with His touch (Matthew 8:1–4). He did so because all life is valuable and irreplaceable. This true value of all human life is exactly what these two paramedics failed to understand.

Similarly, in the first century of the Common Era, shepherds were on the lowest rung on the social ladder. They lived outside with their sheep and smelled no different. Because of their occupation they were basically society's outcasts and no strangers to loneliness. The way these shepherds were viewed 2000 years ago might be similar to how the homeless are viewed today. These would be the people who you and I pass each day who we would rather *not* know. But God wanted to introduce them to His newborn Son.

They had no expensive instruments or training which allowed the wise men to follow Jesus' star in the East. Yet, God wanted them at the grand birthday party of His Son, so He sent heavenly angels to deliver their invitation. They probably wished to have the vast resources of the wise men. Maybe they wanted to also give a lavish gift to give their King, like the affluent visitors did. But their mere presence was gift-enough for the Savior to accept. The same is true today.

Maybe you also wish you had something more to give God than the little in your possession. He knows this and He understands your heart's desire. However, don't think your lack of resources in anyway disqualifies you from serving the Lord. To the contrary, Jesus is not looking for those with overflowing bank accounts to serve Him; He is looking for those with overflowing *hearts* to serve Him. The shepherds left Bethlehem and told the *entire countryside* about the Christ. Meanwhile the Bible says the wise (and rich) men left Bethlehem *telling nobody* about the Christ (see Matthew 2:12).

So if you are considered poor in today's society, don't be ashamed of your circumstances. There is good news for you! Mary proclaimed, the Lord ". . . has put down the mighty from *their* thrones, and exalted *the* lowly. He has filled *the* hungry with good things, and *the* rich He has sent away empty" (Luke 1:52–53, NKJV). It is *you*, not the rich, who will be honored with the tremendous privilege of proclaiming the good news of Jesus Christ to the world. As you follow God's leading through your troubling time, you will discover that you and I, the poor of this world, are the Lord's choice servants!

The manger-scene was also meant to be a sign for the shepherds (Matthew 2:12). A sign in the Bible is generally reserved for something unusual and unexpected in daily life. To find a newborn baby in a hospital's prenatal care unit would not be much of a sign, because we *expect* this. But an angel announcing the birth of a baby in *an animal-shed* was considered a *real sign*! So, when the shepherds arrived to find baby Jesus in a feeding trough, they were filled with great awe and wonder. However, this sign cost Mary and Joseph the convenience and comfort of a typical birth-process. There was no room for them at the inn, and there was no help for them in life.

Today there is not much room at the "prosperity inn" either. If you are like me, you never even made it in the door. Don't feel bad; Joseph and Mary didn't either. Maybe you are not seeing a "miracle door" open for you. Neither did Mary and Joseph. Nevertheless, God wants you to trust Him through your hard times, because He has a plan for you through it. Just like Mary and Joseph, *your purpose in life cannot be separated from your trials.* These two elements are hard-linked together. To split the two apart would be to destroy both. Further, just like this ancient couple, *out of your most trying time and your greatest darkness will come your greatest blessing in life.* Maybe right now you are "birthing" the fulfillment of your destiny, and you didn't even know it!

The circumstances which are forcing you into transition are the early rumblings of God's answer to your long-awaited request. After praying for your destiny for years, even decades, you probably thought God was ignoring you. But He wasn't. He was listening to every syllable, just like I listen to every Christmas-list request of my son and choose the best toy for him. Similarly, God has been making intricate preparations for the ultimate fulfillment of your big-ticket request.

Moreover, often the Lord's answers come in ways we do not expect. For example, for the last decade or more I have known that God called me to ministry. However, even after finishing seminary I could not find a ministry position. Doors just did not open for me. This was a frustrating two-year period for me, especially since I was barely making a four-digit income per year to support my family.

However, it was during these difficult times when I began to write this book to help others through similar circumstances. I never hoped to launch my writing career by spending two years living at half the poverty level. But without such trials, this book would have never been written. To my displeasure, God arranged for my conditions to be conducive to writing this book. Now I am thankful He did (and I am honored you are reading it).

What I am saying is this: your long-time big-ticket prayer request is *right now being answered*! As with Mary and Joseph, your greatest blessing is waiting for you at the darkest point of your trials. And the fact that your trials have begun is *proof* that ultimate fulfillment of your destiny is just around the corner. Life doesn't get much more exciting than it is *right now*!

However, it is understandable if you are not appreciating this trying time. You might even think life kind of stinks. Nevertheless, *don't give-up*, regardless of your feelings. Although Mary and Joseph did not realize it, in the midst of their darkest hour came the greatest light the world would ever see. Similarly, you may not understand how this dark and difficult time is leading you towards your bright future, *but it is*. You may not see the gears in motion to bring something beautiful and life-giving into your bosom, *but they are*.

Just like Joseph and Mary, the greatest blessing of your life will come out of the great distress you are experiencing right now. God has not forgotten you. To the contrary, He has been protecting you and providing for you every day. He has even been working to *exceed* your expectations. He wants to *surprise* you, just like I try to surprise my son at Christmastime. And as Jesus once said, "If you then, being evil, know how to give good gifts to your children, how much more will your Father who is in heaven give good things to those that ask Him!"(Matthew 7:11, NKJV). The Lord has good plans for you and He is actively working to fulfill your big-ticket prayer and ultimate destiny, and nothing and no one can hinder it! Nonetheless, it will take some effort and some pain to bring it to fruition. If you can endure the difficulty just a little longer you will receive your greatest blessing ever, and when it happens you will quickly forget the pain associated with its delivery. Mary did, and so will you.

Discussion Questions

1. Can you give an example of how you (or others) who used to make decisions based on positive motivations are now making decisions based on negative circumstances? How has this transition affected you personally?

2. Have you recently felt like you did something wrong and God is punishing you? Why or why not? What should you do about it?

3. Is it possible that God is trying to get you to a certain place, and that He is using your negative circumstances to get you there? How so?

4. Has this type of leading from God disrupted your expectations of how you expect the Lord to lead you?

5. Have you, in honesty, expected a "flowery bed of roses" to carry you through life? Has this expectation been recently changed? Explain.

6. Is it possible that your future is linked to your uncomfortable transition? Explain.

7. What "interesting arrangements" (like living with your in-laws) have you been forced into because of your circumstances? Can you identify the benefits of such arrangements?

8. How can you be sure God will direct every detail of your life to ensure everything turns-out according to His good plan? What evidence is there to support this concept?

9. Is your life important to God? How do your circumstances affect this? Explain.

10. Can your purpose in life be separated from your trials? Why or why not?

11. What can you expect to be the result of going through your greatest hour of darkness? Explain.

12. Can you imagine that the answer to your long-time, big-ticket prayer request is being answered through your current difficulties? Why or why not?

6

Why Can't I Find a Job?

The Eleventh Hour Worker: God's Hiring Process

(MATTHEW 20:1–16)

*In the day of prosperity we have many refuges to resort to;
in the day of adversity only one.*

—HORATIUS BONAR

I CAN STILL PICTURE the sunny Colorado day when I graduated from high school. I remember smelling the freshly-mowed football field, and walking toward my appointed chair to the tune of "Pomp and Circumstance." My fellow classmates were full of smiles, and my relatives turned-out in spades. As the speaker's words resonated through the crisp mountain air, I found myself watching the lonely cloud-puffs float across the deep blue sky. Needless to say, I don't recall the keynote speaker, but I remember the essence of his speech. He charged me and the other eighty-nine graduates to accept our destiny to change the world for the better. He charged us to seek to help others and better their lives. And as I clutched my diploma I nearly buckled under the weight of my newfound destiny to (da-da-da-daa) . . . *change the world.*

That was several years ago (fifteen to be exact). Since then I've found that changing the world is a little more difficult than it sounds. Don't get me wrong, I've tried. Still, somewhere along the way *life happened,* and I'm just not sure if I'm still up to the task. I mean, changing the world is a pretty tall order, all things considered. Actually, I've been thinking that maybe I should lower my standards a little. Instead of changing *the world,* maybe I could just change *my neighborhood block*. I could organize a yard-sale. We could even sell brownies. People might like that. And I think it would make *the block* a better place. But as for changing *the world*, I'm not so sure if I'm still up for it. Most days I just hope I can *survive* it.

Maybe *life happened* to you, also. If you took a moment, you would probably remember a few specific instances. You didn't ask for it, and you didn't expect it, but it happened anyway. Maybe your marriage began on a wonderful cloud of bliss floating above all troubles. Then your cloud ran into a mountain-sized problem and burst; you have been lonely ever since. Perhaps you achieved wonderful career success, until the company downsized and left you on the street. Or maybe your loved one was diagnosed with a medical condition, the name of which still haunts the corridors of your mind. Every one of us has our own story about when *life happened*. It ripped-out your heart and left you scarred for life. And you're still trying to get over it, go through it, or somehow get on with it. Me too.

So, what do we do when life hasn't turned-out how we hoped? I truly hope life has worked-out for you *far better* than your greatest dreams and wildest expectations! If it has, then I ask that you finish reading this book so you can better understand your underprivileged neighbors, employees, and friends (including me). However, if this book has been speaking to your heart, then maybe you and I really aren't so different. You see, I have discovered that I am not the only one who feels like I haven't lived-up to the high expectations of my high school graduation speech.

I've heard it's lonely at the top. I wouldn't know. But I know it feels lonely at the bottom. When life turns against you it's easy to feel like you're at the bottom of the pile. And not many people want to be your friend when you're at the bottom. The church is the *one place* on the planet where poor folks are supposed to be honored above the rich (see James 1:9–11, 2:1–9). In reality, however, its social aspects are often structured no differently than the world's class-based system.

But there is good news for those of us who rank last in life. After all, the first part of the Lord Jesus Christ's "Magna Charta" was to proclaim good news to the poor (see Luke 4:18). As part of this good news, Jesus later declared that God has a plan to play the old "switcheroo" trick on mankind's pecking order: "But many *who are* first will be last, and the last first" (Matthew 19:30, NKJV).

Right after Jesus gave this cryptic saying, He launched into a lengthy parable about a landowner who went out to hire workers for his vineyard. Obviously this was meant to shed light on Jesus' saying, but for most of us it does more to *cloud* the meaning than to *clarify* it. Maybe it's a mystery because the hiring process in America today isn't quite as simple and observable as it was 2000 years ago. Today we just don't see groups of people standing outside super-stores waiting to be hired as fruit-pickers for the day. So we're going to rewind 2000 years of history and immerse ourselves in the life of this parable to better understand it. Ready? Let's listen to Jesus tell His parable:

> For the kingdom of heaven is like a landowner who went out early in the morning to hire laborers for his vineyard. Now when he had agreed with the laborers for a denarius a day, he sent them into his vineyard. And he went out about the third hour and saw others standing idle in the marketplace, and said to them, "You also go into the vineyard, and whatever is right I will give you." So they went. Again he went out about the sixth and the ninth hour, and did likewise. And about the eleventh hour he went out and found others standing idle, and said to them, "Why have you been standing here idle all day?" They said to him, "Because no one hired us." He said to them, "You also go into the vineyard, and whatever is right you will receive." (Matthew 20:1–7, NKJV)

You wake up at 5:30AM and head out, anxious to do some honest hard work. After your brisk ½-mile walk to the market, you make your way to the hiring area. Today there are many workers for hire, you notice. You calculate that there must be at least twenty, and more keep arriving. This troubles you slightly; your family is counting on you to make a full day's wage. You wonder: will there be enough work for everybody? But you push this concern aside. God knows you need the work; He will help you find a job today. If you can get a few weeks of solid employment, you might be able to put-away a little money for your taxes which are soon due. Within half an hour, three employers arrive, and each chooses a couple men. This is a good sign. Even though they didn't pick you, the employers seem anxious to bring-in their harvests, so they are hiring liberally. Pretty soon another employer comes, then another. Things are looking up.

You keenly observe the workers' reactions every time an employer walks through this portion of the market. The men instantly stand tall and puff-up their chests. They know employers only take the biggest and strongest workers. Size is one means to convince a potential employer of their expected productivity. But you are one of the smallest. No matter how much you straighten-up and hold your breath, you still cannot compare to the broad shoulders of the others. Regardless, God knows you need the work; God will help.

You also watch the employers. Each one glides through the marketplace with eyes darting. They are all shrewd in their own way, but in essence they are all the same. After a few encounters, you know their routine probably better than they do. You can tell a landowner even from a distance, by the authority and swagger in his gate. With a calculating eye he inspects each potential worker, all the while taking mental notes. A muscular specimen peaks his business interest. One eyebrow lifts and a half-smile flashes across his face. A slight nod of approval conveys his thoughts: "This one might bring-in four extra bushels today." Then he motions the candidate to follow him, and he turns to walk away. The hire has been made. You have seen this scenario played-out this morning several times already. Still, you continue to stand among the crowd of those waiting for an opportunity. The day is still early, and hope is still high. Your time is coming, and God knows you need the work.

The next employer approaches. He sees you. For a fleeting moment your eyes meet. But he quickly turns, breaking the glance. His half-smile fades, and the wrinkles around his eyes relax. Clearly he is unimpressed by your size. He again looks at the larger man across from you and motions for him to follow. You don't get the job . . . again. Rejection is slowly becoming a part of you. More employers are coming, you tell yourself. There is still hope. God knows you need the work. God knows . . .

A few hours go by, with only a few other employers walking through. The sun is hot today, and you're not standing as tall as you were this morning. You find a rock and sit-down to wait for another employer. Time passes. Your shoulders slouch to a more relaxed position. As the sun lowers in the sky, your hope follows. At least one employer has come back a couple times. Here he is again! You quickly stand up—this might be your chance! But he chooses another and they walk away together. With each passing hour hope fades more. God knows . . .

You've watched the day away, and now there are just a couple more hours until 6pm, the end of the workday. Reality sets-in, and you realize that if you don't get a job *today*, your family will not eat *tomorrow*. God *does* know, doesn't He? With the passing of the next hour you begin to accept the fact that you will come home with nothing. Third time this week. What will you tell the kids? Life is becoming more of a burden than a blessing. *Does* God care? Surely nobody else will make a hire today, so you might as well leave, you figure. But still, you stay. It's not that you actually expect to get a job so late in the day, but rather, you are too ashamed to go home early with nothing to show. After all, *you* are the family provider. How can you *again* tell your wife and children that they won't eat again tomorrow? And how can you convince them God will provide, when you're not convinced yourself? All you can do is pray for a miracle.

Then one of the employers returns to the market again. This time you don't bother to stand. There is no reason to. He sees you again, just as he saw you the other times he walked through. But this time something different happens: *he looks at you.* Then the unspeakable happens—he *approaches* you. "Why haven't you worked today?" he asks. You answer off-the-cuff, "Nobody has hired me." He motions with his hand, "Go to work in my vineyard." You feel a lump in your throat. Your prayer has been answered! You follow him to a vineyard where you begin picking grapes. How much will he pay? Don't know. Surely you won't receive a full-day's wage, but maybe you will earn enough to feed the children, at least. You can fast for another day, but the children can't—in order to grow, they need to eat. So you trust him. You have no other choice but to trust him.

At this point, I want to break away from the story to ask you a personal question: do you feel like the world has rejected you? How many rejection letters have you received from potential employers lately? You diligently apply to position after position, only to learn it has already been filled. Or maybe you do actually get an interview. Dressed to impress, you firmly shake hands and sit across the table from your interviewers. You confidently answer their questions one after another with poise and clarity. In your own mind, you *nailed* those questions. And you should have—you rehearsed in the mirror for an *entire week.* But days later one more rejection letter tops your stack. What went wrong *this* time? You were *perfect* for that job! If God is on your side, then why is nobody *else* on it?

If somebody would only give you a chance, you would work twice as hard to prove yourself. You would show them you're the best person for the job. You'd work extra hours to ensure your position. But you'll never even have the *opportunity.* You have been passed over. You've been rejected—*again.*

Employment rejections can be based on any number of things. Maybe they think you're not smart enough. Oh, but they'd never actually *say* that to you. But if you recall, one interviewer did seem to have a condescending tone towards you. Or, perhaps you were not rejected based upon intelligence, but upon *appearance*. Your resume was head and shoulders above the rest, making you the leading candidate for the job. That is, until another applicant promenaded through the doors with a seductive miniskirt and low neckline. Shortly thereafter, you were determined to be "over-qualified" and thereby dismissed.

Possibly your rejection was because you're not American enough. Anybody who speaks with a foreign accent knows this discrimination well. Or maybe it was because you're not experienced enough or not young enough. An older friend of mine on the job hunt commented, "Employers want a thirty-year old with thirty years of experience." There is much truth in this. Regardless of the specific reasons for your rejection, the reality is that everybody can connect with the feeling, because *we have all been there*. This is why all of us can relate with the laborer who was passed-by time and again. Life supplies rejection in abundance, but acceptance is rare.

This parable is a visualization of how different people (portrayed as the laborers) relate to God (portrayed as the employer/landowner), and vice-versa. The eleventh-hour worker is the person who feels that nothing goes their way. They are constantly forced to swim upstream in life, and can't help but wonder why God does not open doors of opportunity for *them*. Instead, doors usually slam in their face. These were the first to lose their job when the cutbacks hit, and they have been waiting the longest to find another position. They are not looking for an *entitlement*, but only an *opportunity*. Often, life is not much fun for these folks. *I* am an eleventh-hour worker, and maybe you are one, too. For us, the implied exhortation of this parable is a simple one: *don't give-up*. As long as there is daylight there is hope. You may have to wait longer than you would like. You might even have to out-wait your amount of hope, but *if you will wait*, a door of opportunity *will* open to you.

However, there is more. Your particular door of opportunity just might surprise you. The principle here is one which God spoke to my wife several months ago. After finishing my seminary degree I expected doors to swing wide-open for me in my new career field. But they did not. So I expanded my job-search to related areas for which I was also well-qualified. Yet I still received rejections. So I expanded my search to include nearly *any* type of job, still with no success. Once I even applied to a position which entailed little more than putting tape on library books, and *I didn't even get an interview*! Disappointment doesn't begin to describe how badly I felt through that process. In the midst of this intense sadness, God communicated a powerful and timely truth to my wife: *if nobody hires you, then* God *will hire you.*

You see, sometimes God calls a person into His service *because* they have already been rejected by every other industry. Other times the Lord *recruits* a person into ministry by closing all of the other doors which they have been knocking on. As an example, the only reason why I began writing this book was because I lost my own part-time minimum-wage job, and I couldn't find another. And since nobody *else* would hire me, *God* hired me to write for Him. And it has been a great honor and privilege to do so.

If you have recently lost your job, don't be dismayed. This might be God's way of promoting you out of an unworthy company and into His worthy service. If you think about it, you really didn't lose much when they handed you the pink slip. If you were still stuck in that old job, then God would not be able to navigate you into the new place in life where He wants you. But now you are at His disposal, and He will lead you to His choice of positions for you. When it happens, it will be a real blessing for you (and others) in many ways. Sometimes you have to leave the place of "it's good enough" to find your promised land.

I don't know what companies your rejection letters came from, but I think they did you a favor by sending those letters. I know it can be disheartening to receive another rejection, but it is for the best. Many of these companies are not worthy of your time, talent, or your effort. At some of those businesses the management mistreats and degrades their workers. There may be no room for advancement because of back-stabbing office politics. And to top it off, some of these companies are infamous for underpaying their employees. *Thank God* you didn't get those jobs! God has something much better for you. He will hire you *for Himself*!

This just might be the time when God calls *you* into *ministry*! Maybe God allowed all of those other doors to close in your face just so you would be undistracted by other endeavors and ready to accept this higher calling. If this is the case with you, then it is important to note that ministry can come in many forms. It can be a full-time job, as with church staff members. But most often ministry is done as a bi-vocational venture, in which you work a normal job to support yourself financially, and meanwhile make the effort to still serve others. The Apostle Paul did this. He supported himself by making tents while he evangelized the known world. Additionally, there are many *specific ways* to minister to others, including through speaking, administrating, singing, and a hundred other possibilities. One friend of mine started a physical fitness ministry to teach others how to take better care of their bodies. Ministry possibilities are endless!

As you have been searching and waiting for a job, God has been walking through the marketplace looking for people to work in His world-wide vineyard. And my friend, *He has noticed you.* Possibly, just when you think all hope is gone, He will stroll through your life again, and call you to the perfect ministry for you. And you'll be *thrilled* to follow!

Jesus continued His parable:

> So when evening had come, the owner of the vineyard said to his steward, "Call the laborers and give them *their* wages, beginning with the last to the first." And when those came who *were hired* about the eleventh hour, they each received a denarius. But when the first came, they supposed that they would receive more; and they likewise received each a denarius. And when they had received *it,* they complained against the landowner, saying, "These last *men* have worked *only* one hour, and you made them equal to us who have borne the burden and the heat of the day." But he answered one of them and said, "Friend, I am doing you no wrong. Did you not agree with me for a denarius? Take *what is* yours and go your way. I wish to give to this last man *the same* as to you. Is it not lawful for me to do what I wish with my own things? Or is your eye evil because I am good?" So the last will be first, and the first last. For many are called, but few chosen (Matthew 20:8–16, NKJV).

Imagine the elation of the last-hired workers as their reward was placed in their hands. They looked down to discover that they each received a *full day's wage!* This was far more than they had hoped for. Remember, those hired last had only a one-sided work agreement (see Matthew 20:7). They had *no idea* what their recompense would be. It is one thing to work for a predetermined pay, but quite another to labor with no stated compensation.

It can be uncomfortable to work for an undisclosed reward, as you never really know how you will come-out in the end. Likewise, it can be difficult to trust God when there is no predetermined benefit. After all, we don't really understand what the end result will be. However, when you are out of options, the only thing you can do is trust His goodness and integrity. In this parable, these workers were forced to trust the integrity and goodness of the landowner. In doing so, however, they set themselves up for a blessing. Likewise, when we trust God's integrity and goodness, we prepare ourselves to be blessed, also.

You see, if you make a contract, then you will be paid the agreed-upon wage which you worked to earn. But if your labor for God is based upon trust, He won't necessarily pay you what you earned, because you may only have *earned* a little. Instead, He will *give* you (as a gift) more than you deserve and more than you expect (see Matthew 20:4). In this parable, the reward for those hired later was based on the *landowner's generosity*, not the *laborer's productivity*. Likewise, when your labor for God is founded upon trust, your reward will not be based upon your productivity in life or religion, but on His *benevolent kindness*. This parable makes it clear that *God's nature is to bless those who trust His integrity and goodness with more than they expect.*

However, there is another party in this parable to consider: the workers hired *first*. These workers complained against the gracious nature of the landowner. Human nature hasn't changed in 2000 years, so you can expect there to be people who protest against the gracious things which God accomplishes in *your* life. They don't think you are *qualified* for it, they don't feel you have *earned* it, and they certainly don't believe you *deserve* it. Interestingly enough, however, in their minds they themselves meet all three of these criteria. They toiled and sweated to get to where they are in life, and they don't like the thought of you being *handed* that which they worked so hard to *earn*. These folks cannot yet truly understand the grace which freely gives a salvation which could never be earned.

These people will also complain because *they did not see it coming*. They looked at you and judged you according to your outward appearance. "S/he is a nobody and will never amount to anything," they calculated. I have received this condemnation from no less than a distinguished seminary professor, and *it hurt*. Similarly, you have probably endured such judgments also. The fact is, however, if it weren't for God's grace, these critics would be 100% correct. No doubt about it. *But God's grace makes them dead wrong.* You did not earn it, and you really don't deserve it, but if you trust God, He will give you the blessing anyway. This is how grace works. As Christians, we obey God and labor for Him. But this is not to put the Lord in debt to us, as "payment for services" would indicate. He owes us nothing for *any* of our efforts (see Luke 17:10). Instead, we obey and labor for God simply because *we love Him.* Yet in the end, He still *rewards* us because of His generosity.

In this parable, the master ordered the steward to pay the eleventh-hour workers in the presence of the workers hired first. The master could have been much more discrete in his method of disbursement. Today, this might even be characterized as "business sense." But he chose not to. In fact, he made it a point to openly pay the same amount to all workers, *from last to first.* The landowner *wanted* the other workers to *see* his generosity in action. This wasn't to boast, however. It was to *reveal their arrogant attitudes.*

Similarly, God will not hide your blessings from your critics. In fact, He will go *out of His way* to make sure *they see* what He has done for you. God *wants* others to see His goodness and grace in action through *your* life. And He intends to use your blessing to confront *and correct* the prideful attitudes of others. The same people who have written-off you and your future will eat their words—God will make sure of it! You won't even have to defend yourself. When they grumble against God's blessings in your life, they are really grumbling against the Lord's generous nature. As with the parable, when this happens, the Lord Himself will defend His actions and correct the offender.

The "last will be first" principle is both an exhortation and a warning. It is a stern warning for Christians who think they have "earned" something from God, to stop trusting their works, and to start trusting God's kindness. Additionally, it is an encouraging exhortation for underdog Christians to trust God and thereby receive an over-comer's reward. Nobody knows exactly when this pecking-order exchange will take place. Personally, I believe the major switch will happen in heaven, but I also think there are key moments in a Christian's life when God decides to either promote or demote an individual based on their attitudes (a "mini-assessment" of sorts). However, regardless of when or how it happens, you can be sure that the "old switcheroo trick" will indeed happen.

Concerning your situation today, if you still can't find a job, don't give-up. Keep trying and keep waiting, even though all hope may fade away. If nobody else will hire you, then God Himself will bring you into His field of service. He is still in the business of hiring people who others consider valueless, and then paying them more than they deserve. You won't get a better offer than that with *any* company. And if this financial crisis is God's way of calling you, then you are indeed blessed. This is the beginning of the most exciting time of your life! God will lead you into the right field for you to labor in, and you will be overjoyed and honored to be a minister of the Most High God. Even further, by God's grace, you *will* live-up to your high school graduation speech. You *will* change the world and make it a better place . . . one life at a time.

Discussion Questions

1. Describe an instance of when "life happened" to you. How has this incident affected you since it happened?

2. Do you "connect" with the story of the worker who could not find a job? How so and in what ways?

3. How have you felt rejected by the world?

4. Do you feel as though you might be an "eleventh-hour worker"? Why or why not?

5. What might God do if nobody else will hire you? How would this look if it were to happen?

6. What would your reaction be if God called you into His service, as a result of your hardships?

7. When someone works for God, what does He base their "reward" upon? Why?

8. How might others react to God distributing your "reward" for service? Why?

9. Does God ever really "owe" us anything? Explain.

10. What does "the last will be first" mean to you?

7

But I'm a Nobody

Abel: God Honors Insignificant People

(Genesis 4:1–15)

*The good are made better by ill, as odours crushed
are sweeter still.*

—Samuel Rogers

I FOUND MYSELF SEATED in front of the leader of the organization. He leaned towards me to ask what programs I would implement if given the opportunity. It felt as though his gaze would penetrate my very soul. I realized there were papers in my hand, and without a word I passed them across his large desk. With only slight interest, he quickly flipped through the first few sheets. Then something caught his eye. His pace slowed and he began to closely examine each remaining page. With a pleased look he neatly placed the packet on the desk and leaned back in his chair. Our eyes met once again and I *knew* I had made the team.

Just as he was about to assign me to a small management role, a familiar assistant entered the office and moved quickly to his side. This person whispered into his ear, and within an instant the room's atmosphere changed drastically. The leader's eyes narrowed and his expression of pleasant surprise shifted to one of skepticism and disapproval. Before I understood what was happening, I had been dismissed from the room. Nothing more was spoken.

Although it was only a dream, I understood what God was conveying to me through it: *slander killed my opportunity.* This interpretation rang true. Although I was well-qualified for a management role, during my five years at that organization I was never again considered for one.

Why isn't life fair? Sometimes our hopes and dreams (even God-given ones) can be completely destroyed, never to be fulfilled. This can happen because of our own poor decisions, as God doesn't always shield us from the consequences of our bad choices. However, a dream can also be shattered by a shrewd antagonist, like mine was. You probably have a similar story of your own.

Maybe you witnessed an authority figure cruelly mistreat someone, and become frustrated when you discovered there was no way to remove the victim to a safer environment. Or maybe *you* were the one who was callously wronged. You paid your dues to the company through years of faithful service, proving that you deserve a greater role. You should have gotten the promotion—you earned it. Nevertheless, a coworker's brutal smear campaign derailed your opportunity, and scuttled your entire career. And you have been stuck in the same low-level position ever since. *Everybody* has a heart-wrenching story of the good guy losing, justice not being served, or irreversible tragedy happening to the least deserving. And we all wonder, "why does God allow it?"

For years I made-believe these occurrences never happened. I reasoned that a just God would not allow such permanent tragedies to happen to His children. I figured the just Lord would somehow "fix" each and every one of these situations. Surely God would turn the situation around and direct the antagonist's misdeeds upon himself, I trusted. But the truth is, sometimes this justice never happens on earth. Sometimes God just stands back and does nothing while the wrongdoing happens. And after watching and personally experiencing such injustices, I can no longer "pretend them away." Further, I am tired of the "easy-cheesy" answer that says everything will turn-out alright, because *sometimes it doesn't*. There are some situations which *nothing* can fix. Sadly, there are times when it seems that *sin* really does *win*.

In fact, it is so sadly *uncommon* for the underdog to win, that when it *actually happens* Hollywood makes a movie about it! Don't get me wrong, these true stories are wonderful, and in my opinion, they make the best films. I love movies like *Chariots of Fire*, *The Rookie*, and other similar true stories. But if it is *normal* for the good guy to prevail in everyday life, then why are there so few "based on a true story" films about it *actually happening*? We are so used to the good girl finishing *last* that when we actually *see* a true depiction of her *winning*, our emotions kick-into high gear, and we cheer and cry at the same time! If good *normally* prevailed in everyday life, then there would be no reason to make movies about it. Such "based on a true story" movies often do well because they do not depict the norm; they depict the *exception*.

One argument against the existence of the Christian God is based upon this very concept. The classical statement of the argument goes like this: if God were benevolent (all-good) He would *want to* eliminate all evil; if God were omnipotent (all-powerful) He *could* eliminate all evil; therefore, since evil remains, then God cannot be both benevolent and omnipotent. Those who subscribe to this logic use the existence of evil in today's world in their attempt to disprove the existence of a sovereign and benevolent God. However, as Christians we believe God is both of these things. So, the question remains: why does evil still exist? Or, as stated in our initial question, *why is life not fair*?

We will never know the complete answer this side of heaven, but we can gain some understanding by examining the world's first family feud. Let's take a look: "Now Adam knew Eve his wife, and she conceived and bore Cain, and said, 'I have acquired a man from the LORD.' Then she bore again, this time his brother Abel. Now Abel was a keeper of sheep, but Cain was a tiller of the ground" (Genesis 4:1–2, NKJV).

Adam and Eve were the first couple in the human race. They were the *great* grandparents of you and me both. However, beyond their creation and their fall, most of us know very little about them. So, we are going to piece-together information from the Bible to get an up-close and personal look at their lives. Nevertheless, please remember there were no video cameras at the dawn of mankind to capture the scene exactly as it was, so we will merely do our best to recreate the first family scene. With this in mind, please step back in time several thousands of years and meet your great, great, great, great, *great* grand-family.

First we have great Grandpa Adam, a farmer. He has worked the ground ever since he was formed *from* it, which fact makes him pretty special. However, his job got a lot tougher when he and his wife got kicked out of the celebrated Garden of Eden, and so did *he*. His portion of the curse included sweaty labor to produce fruit from the ground (Genesis 3:19). In the good-old days, plants and trees used to spring-up on their own. But after Adam and Eve's "big mistake," it took much more work to grow *anything*. Accordingly, Grandpa Adam spent plenty of time in the fields. He was probably out there from sun-up to sun-down, tilling and sowing and reaping and threshing. This made him a pretty tough man. You have to be strong to farm, but you have to be *really* strong to do it for centuries (people back then lived much longer than we do today). He was good at it, too. Maybe it came from his personal roots, but *nobody* knew farming like Grandpa Adam.

Grandma Eve was something special, also. Although she was initially the only woman on the face of the planet, it was also certain she was *gorgeous*. Well, Adam thought so, anyway. The instant Grandpa Adam laid eyes on her he intuitively knew that she was the *perfect match* for him. In fact, he was so excited that he married her *that same day!* And she must have been just as tough as she was beautiful. While Adam was out in the fields all day, Grandma Eve was busy running the household. Every farmer knows that a farmer's wife works just as hard in the home as her husband does in the field. It is certain Eve was a good helper to Adam in farming *and* in raising their family.

Speaking of the children, their first was a son. It is possible that Grandpa Adam wasn't around for the actual birth moment, because Grandma Eve was the one who named him. She was so excited to have received a man-child from the Lord that she called him *Cain*. According to the late biblical Hebrew expert Heinrich Fredrich Wilhelm Gesenius, "Cain" basically means *obtained*.[4] The fact is they truly *had* acquired something special: the world's first bouncing baby boy. They could hardly be prouder.

However, then along came their second child *Abel*. Abel was also a boy, but he was not like Cain. He was different. He was probably smaller and weaker. Grandpa Adam and Grandma Eve were apparently underwhelmed with this frail little child, possibly Cain's twin, because they simply called him *Abel*, which (according to Mr. Gesenius) denotes "something vain and empty"; or in today's language, *worthless*.[5]

Clearly Abel was of little importance to Adam and Eve; meanwhile Cain was their pride and joy. Cain even followed in his daddy's footsteps by becoming a farmer. Every father feels a deep sense of satisfaction when his son follows in his footsteps, so there was a close affinity between the father and son. Cain was surely strong just like his daddy. He would have to be as tough as nails to continue the family business for the next several centuries. Cain had a special place in the hearts of Grandpa Adam and Grandma Eve.

Nevertheless, they sure didn't feel the same bond with their second son, *Worthless*. Can you imagine what it would be like to be called this as your name *every single day of your entire life*? "Hey Worthless—if I've told you once, I've told you a thousand times, stay away from the fire!" Or, "Worthless, go get some water, and be quick about it for *once*." Poor little Worthless just could not measure-up to *the great Cain* in the aspects of life which were important to his mother and father. I'm sure he tried his best to work as hard as Cain, or to be as strong or as smart as Cain. Still, no matter how hard he tried, he could not live-up to the standard which Cain set. The bar was just too high for him.

Please don't misunderstand; the Bible does not indicate that Abel *was* useless; it only indicates that his parents *thought* he was useless, since he was *different*. Many parents today realize that each child is unique, and special in their own way. After all, siblings are never carbon copies of each other, nor should they be. It is alright to be different. In fact, differences are *good*. Differences add spice and flavor to an otherwise monochrome existence. They make life interesting and fun. But Grandpa and Grandma didn't understand this, and so they just couldn't truly accept Abel as he was. Honestly, it would be hard for us to blame them. After all, they were farmers, not psychiatrists. However, decade upon decade (possibly even century after century) of this negative attention took a toll on the younger son, and he probably withdrew from family-life. Being alone was his only escape from the pain.

Maybe you have experienced this form of negative attention, also. Your parents might have unfairly compared you to a sibling, a family friend, or even themselves. Maybe your family was ashamed that your musical talent wasn't what they hoped. Or maybe you didn't measure-up to others' athletic prowess, or had difficulty with math in school. Regardless of the specific area, your parents never intended to wound you emotionally. Yet it still happened, and it has affected much of your life.

Even though those around you may have never noticed it, you are truly your own person. You are unique and talented in your own way. Although others may not be able to appreciate what you have to offer the world, your contribution is still valid and important. Moreover, there is One who knows every one of your strengths and weaknesses, and He still accepts you just exactly as you are. The principle is this: *even though your earthly parents neither understood your differences nor accepted your contributions to this world, your heavenly Father does.* God made you to be *different*, and He did it *on-purpose*. He is not in the business of making drones or replicas. Drones are boring and replicas have no value. The Mona Lisa is worth hundreds of millions of dollars; its replica is worth only a few bucks. Similarly, God made you to be *unique*. And as long as you are unique, you are *valuable*. Further, God wants *you* to be the one who adds spice and flavor to the lives of those around you. This won't happen if you are a drone.

Worthless-Abel would leave the family for long periods of time, possibly using the excuse, "well, *somebody* needs to watch the sheep" in order to get away from the constant barrage of degradation. Or maybe the family felt uncomfortable with him around, so they sent him out to watch the sheep for months at a time. In biblical times, shepherding was not considered a high-brow occupation. Families did *not* send-out their pride-and-joy to live an isolated life of caring for filthy sheep; they sent the family *runt*. Much later Israel's King David was found in similar circumstances (see 1 Samuel 16:11). The last of eight brothers, David was not even considered important enough to be invited to the family party. He may not have been named "Worthless," but David was treated like it. His and Abel's family lives were not so different in this respect. While tending to the sheep, Worthless probably learned the same truths which inspired King David to write the familiar *Shepherd's Psalm,* which begins: "The LORD is my shepherd; I shall not want" (Psalm 23:1, NKJV). I believe it was in this setting that *Abel met God.*

If you, like Abel, have been shunned by family or friends, you are closer to God than you realize. God is near to the brokenhearted (Psalm 34:18), and He is a father of the fatherless (Psalm 68:5). The Lord actively seeks those who have been rejected in life. Lift up your eyes; He is closer than you think. He is waiting to reveal Himself to you in tender ways that heal your heart and restore your joy. Even if nobody else in the world wants to be your friend, *Jesus does.* The Lord Himself will call you His friend (John 15:15), and God the Father will be your loving heavenly Father (Romans 8:15–16), just like with Abel.

Abel's entire family knew about God. His parents had been God-worshippers ever since the Garden days. They weren't perfect, but they never veered from devotion to their Creator. However, there's a vast difference between knowing *about* God, and *knowing God.* It is like the difference between having rink-side seats at a hockey game, and being on the ice during one. The *distance* may be minimal, but the *difference* is tremendous. With one the individual is a *bystander*, while with the other the person is a *participant*.

Knowing God requires an investment in a two-way relationship. Time and communication are essential, as with any successful relationship. If a person were to spend no time with their spouse, their relationship would be ultimately doomed to failure. However, if the individual nurtures the marriage relationship by spending time with their spouse, the relationship will grow and blossom. The concept is the same in our relationship with God. God doesn't want to be our afterthought; He wants to be our *every*-thought. And Worthless-Abel had plenty of time to spend with God while watching sheep graze the quiet, green hills. It was probably during this time when Abel heard God speak loving words of acceptance to him. When Abel heard God communicate His love, approval, and ultimate delight in him just the way he was, he probably broke-down in sobs. Many of us have.

Only those who have received a lifetime of unkind remarks can truly appreciate the tremendous power contained in a simple statement like "you are important to me." When spoken by a credible source, these words can be a potent healing balm for an injured heart. If you have felt mistreated or neglected by those who should have cared for you, then God is waiting to restore your heart and your life. You will be as good as new, without defects or deficiencies. You will be *thrilled* with the *new you*, just as Abel was. In addition, you will relate to everything and everybody differently. Abel experienced this healing power as God filled-in the fatherly gaps in his life, and it completely changed how he related to God and life. We see this at the first family's next worship service. "And in the process of time it came to pass that Cain brought an offering of the fruit of the ground to the LORD. Abel also brought of the firstborn of his flock and of their fat. And the LORD respected Abel and his offering, but He did not respect Cain and his offering. And Cain was very angry, and his countenance fell" (Genesis 4:3–5, NKJV).

Most likely this religious service was an annual event, possibly coinciding with the time of harvest. Each son brought a gift they thought God would be pleased with. Or, more accurately, each brought whatever *they* were pleased to give God. The biblical record does not mention the gifts of Adam or Eve, but maybe Cain just followed his dad's example and brought the standard harvest offering. It was "an offering of the fruit of the ground" (Genesis 4:3, NKJV); but it clearly was not the *first* and *best* he had.

The first portion of the crop harvested each season was called the "first-fruits." It would be tempting to use this first portion to throw a grand party, rejoicing that the long-awaited harvest had finally arrived. Nobody knows if this is what Cain did with his first-fruits. However, we do know that Cain *could have* offered his first-fruits to the Lord that day, but he chose not to. In essence, instead of arriving at the party bringing a freshly-cooked meal made from the choices of ingredients, Cain arrived at God's party with his leftovers.

Abel, on the other hand, brought his *first* and his *best*. Specifically, he brought the "firstborn of his flock and of their fat" (Genesis 4:4, NKJV). Today, we often discard the fat from our steaks before we eat the *real* meat, but 8,000 years ago the fat was a delicacy. People *loved* the fat! Therefore, to give this most-desirable portion to God would only happen at a premium cost to the individual. Still, Abel was so thrilled with his relationship with God that he held *nothing* back. His heart probably leaped for joy as he presented to the Lord the finest gift he had.

King David said, "When my father and my mother forsake me, then the LORD will take care of me" (Psalm 27:10, NKJV). Abel understood this concept. After years and years of mistreatment, somebody finally loved Abel unconditionally, and Abel could not help but reciprocate with a heart full of love. The younger son no longer felt like "Worthless-Abel"; now he was "Beloved-of-God-Abel." Further, his new identity caused him to become a passionate and devoted God-worshipper! And everybody saw it—including God.

God's response was earth-shattering to this family: He accepted Abel and his offering, but did not accept Cain's offering or Cain (Genesis 4:4–5). The Bible doesn't tell us exactly how this was made apparent, so we can only speculate. Possibly God sent fire from heaven to consume the pleasing sacrifice (this happened later in the Bible; see 1 Kings 18:38). Or maybe it was some other sign of approval, like the sky's demeanor. We don't know the exact method, but we know for certain that *somehow* God made it crystal clear that Cain's gift was *not good enough* while Abel's was *approved and accepted*. These brother's circumstances had *reversed*. God had honored Abel above Cain. In other words, on this day Abel had been *promoted* by God. Now he was *a somebody*.

Jesus spoke to this when He taught his disciples, "When you are invited, go and sit down in the lowest place, so that when he who invited you comes he may say to you, 'Friend, go up higher.' Then you will have glory in the presence of those who sit at the table with you" (Luke 14:10, NKJV). To be promoted by God is every Abel's *guaranteed future* (whether in this life or in heaven), and every Cain's *elusive dream*. The reason for this is because *humility is a prerequisite to promotion*. While some are busy scheming and clambering their way to the top, they do not realize that it is those exact efforts which have *disqualified* them from God's advancement process. God only promotes those who humble themselves, like the guest who took the lowest position in Jesus' teaching.

In way of application, this translates into *good news* for anybody who has been kicked-around by life and circumstances. The principle is this: *God loves to promote the weak over the powerful*. It's like a habit He can't kick! God's greatness is seen when He takes somebody who society considers worthless, and forges them into a God-ordained powerhouse for the whole world to see (see Luke 20:17). If you have received the short end of the stick throughout life, then *you* are a prime candidate for promotion. If you will continue to humble yourself, then sooner or later you also will receive this honor which comes from God alone, just as Abel did.

There couldn't be a greater contrast than that between Abel and Cain at that instant. The lifelong Worthless-Abel had been honored for the very first time. Meanwhile, the celebrated golden-boy-Cain had just received his first taste of rejection. This rejection was but a teaspoon-full of that which his little brother had shouldered every single day of his life. However, even one small measure was more than Cain could bear, and he became *livid*.

Have you ever known somebody who always had to *outdo* you? I call these individuals *power-brokers*. They might be a neighbor, a schoolmate, or a coworker; however, they are probably not a friend. Not a *real* friend, anyway. Real friends value each other and exhibit a mutual respect for one another. In contrast, power-brokers have no interest in sincere friendships. Instead, they are consumed with self-promotion, which requires them to assert their supremacy over others. To ensure their dominant position they will lie, slander, or even kill. Cain was a power-broker.

Cain's disapproval by God threw him into a tailspin. With emotions out of control, He felt like he *had* to do something . . . but what? God knew Cain would consider his options sooner or later, so God asked the older brother; "Why are you angry? And why has your countenance fallen? If you do well, will you not be accepted? And if you do not do well, sin lies at the door. And its desire *is* for you, but you shall rule over it" (Genesis 4:6–7, NKJV). This somewhat cryptic saying remains a partial mystery, although at its heart is a stern warning to Cain that *he is responsible before God to control his emotions and actions*. With this dialogue Cain clearly understood that "the devil made me do it" is *never* a valid excuse before God. Although there may be tremendous spiritual temptation to do evil, the individual *always* casts the final authoritative vote on whether to engage in a sin-action, or to flee the enticement.

> Now Cain talked with Abel his brother; and it came to pass, when they were in the field, that Cain rose up against Abel his brother and killed him. Then the Lord said to Cain, "Where *is* Abel your brother?" He said, "I do not know. *Am* I my brother's keeper?" And He said, "What have you done? The voice of your brother's blood cries out to Me from the ground. So now you *are* cursed from the earth, which has opened its mouth to receive your brother's blood from your hand. When you till the ground, it shall no longer yield its strength to you. A fugitive and a vaga- bond you shall be on the earth" (Genesis 4:8–12, NKJV).

Obviously Cain decided that mastery over his feelings was too dif- ficult. Instead, he opted for the "power-broker special": he murdered his brother. Although Cain *was* his "brother's keeper," he never lived-up to the title. Instead, he used the sacred powers entrusted to him (access and confidence) to take his little brother's life. Some ancient manuscripts read that Cain actually *invited* Abel to go into the field with him, indicat- ing Cain had *premeditated* this murderous plot (see Genesis 4:8, NLT). Like a true power-broker, Cain destroyed whatever got in the way of the self-glory which he so badly craved.

To me, the most disturbing aspect of this story is that *Abel died not for wrong-doing, but for right-doing.* He lost his life just after he had been *promoted by God.* Abel did not plan to die early. In fact, he probably had unfulfilled hopes and dreams. Maybe he wanted to marry and start his own family. Or possibly his dream was to increase his flocks so he could give even greater gifts to the Lord. We will never know what these hopes or dreams were, because they died with him. It just *wasn't fair.*

Abel was the very first person to suffered negative consequences for *right*-doing. Adam and Eve suffered for their own sin, but Abel suffered because of the sin of another. Moreover, in the thousands of years since then, nothing has changed. Promoted-Abels still exist, as do power-broker-Cains. Moreover, today's Abels continue to suffer because they possess the *one thing* a Cain can neither earn nor steal: *God's approval.*

Maybe you have suffered loss because of the sin of another. They did not crush your physical body with a raised fist, but they crushed your hopes with deceit. And they didn't end your existence with a weapon, but they scuttled your career with slander. Now you may never reach the position which you were *meant to achieve.* Slander is doing to somebody's reputation what one would rather do to them physically; namely, murder. What I am saying is there is a real possibility that your and my circumstances on this earth will *never* improve. Abel's didn't. Maybe we will never be millionaires, CEO's, or Congress-persons. It would be irresponsible to guarantee that your life will soon become a flowery bed of roses, because for some of us *it will not.* Only God knows our ultimate fates.

This might be a new idea compared to what you have come to expect. At the beginning of your Christian walk, you might have been told that by following Jesus Christ your circumstances would only get better. Yet, in the years since, they have become more difficult. It is possible that you and I will live-out our days in obscure poverty until we quietly slip into eternity. After all, nowhere does the Bible guarantee earthly success or riches for Jesus' followers. In fact, the prominent Christian experience through the last 2,000 years would be more similar to a life of *poverty* than a life of *prosperity.* As we each reluctantly consider that this might be our own reality, it would be easy to assume your life has been a monotonous waste. But that would be a mistake.

The truth is your life has not been inconsequential . . . it has been a *glorious triumph*! Success in life is not measured by your position or your paycheck. Instead, success is measured by *the quality of your character.* Others may not see the trappings of success within you, but God does. With each kind word, and every right and good action you are storing-up for yourself an illustrious brilliance which is too glorious to be revealed on this side of heaven. And the rewards you receive in heaven will *more* than make-up for your years of suffering on earth. The Apostle Paul said it this way: "For I consider that the sufferings of this present time are not worthy *to be compared* with the glory which shall be revealed in us" (Romans 8:18, NKJV). This doesn't just apply to Paul; it applies to you, too.

God never forgets what you do for Him in faith and love, and He will make sure that others remember, also. For example, Abel is the first name mentioned in the illustrious "Hall of Faith" chapter eleven in the Book of Hebrews. It begins, "By faith Abel offered to God a more excellent sacrifice than Cain, through which he obtained witness that he was righteous, God testifying of his gifts; and through it he being dead still speaks" (Hebrews 11:4, NKJV). You see, in *our* eyes, Abel's life ended prematurely, yet his testimony is the longest-lasting one in the Bible. His death continues to proclaim his righteousness, his innocence, and his sacrificial love for God. Thousands of years of commentary on this man has not exhausted the depths of his testimony! And God is no less involved in your life than Abel's.

If you also have quietly suffered mistreatment through life, then don't assume it has been for no reason, or that God has neglected you. You are closer to God's heart than you realize. God's most precious few are the ones who the world seeks to hurt the worst. Because of your devotion to Jesus Christ, you have been honored by God *and* targeted by power-brokers. This is why you have unduly suffered. However, in the end, *your perceived demise will become your greatest testimony.* As impossible as it may sound, your life *with* problems will yield a more powerful testimony than your life *without* problems. Whether your suffering is a ruined reputation, a stunted career, or even a difficult marriage, *God has seen it,* and He will greatly honor you for your faithfulness to Him while you endure it.

Moreover, God Himself is the only true judge of the value of your contribution in life. At the end of your days, you may think you are just another nameless believer, having done nothing worthy of appreciation from the world or acclaim within Christendom. But *you are known of God, and all of heaven admires you.* In his instruction to Timothy the Apostle Paul said, ". . . the good works *of some* are clearly evident, and those that are otherwise cannot be hidden" (1 Timothy 5:25, NKJV). As you innocently follow Abel's example and quietly turn the other cheek to your haters, the Lord will proclaim your life's work of meekness. Further,

God will be sure to deal justly (and often harshly!) with those troubling you (see 2 Thessalonians 1:6). You may not be famous on earth, but you are *an acclaimed celebrity* in eternity.

Although your pain may run deep and long, *continue being faithful to your Lord*, and you will be welcomed into heaven with a grand and glorious celebration. As the Apostle Peter exhorted, "Therefore, brethren, be even more diligent to make your call and election sure, for if you do these things you will never stumble; for so an entrance will be supplied to you abundantly into the everlasting kingdom of our Lord and Savior Jesus Christ" (2 Peter 1:10–11, NKJV). You will shine like the stars, and your days of being an insignificant nobody will forever be over. Most importantly, however, you will forever be in the loving arms of the gentle Lamb of God, Jesus Christ. He has never forgotten His precious servant Abel, and you can be sure He will never forget you, either.

Even though our lives on earth may not get any easier, you and I can take action to *make ourselves* better suited to handle it. You are not responsible for the hand that life deals you, but you *are* responsible for the way you play that hand. You cannot control what comes your way, but you *can* control how you react to it. This is exactly what Section Two of this book is about. Hopefully by now you understand that God truly loves you and He is intimately involved in your life and difficulties. In addition, I expect that by now you have realized that God has specific purposes for you while you are *in* your trials, as one (or more) of these early chapters have resonated with you. *Now* it is time to learn what you can do about it! You must remember, however, our goal is not to end our struggles, but to *better ourselves* while we are going through them. With this in mind, your goal should not be to get out of your trials, but to *use them* to become *a better you*. As you read Section Two of this book, you will learn simple principles and practical methods to strengthen your spiritual life, and improve your emotional life. If you follow these principles and practices, you will regain your footing and traction as a Spirit-led, God-empowered follower of the Lord Jesus Christ!

God has good plans for you, and if you will become an active participant in preparing yourself, then you will find yourself *achieving* those things while your trials diminish in the background. Remember, God is not so concerned with making life better for you; He is interested in making *you* better for life. We are not on earth to vacation; we are on earth to labor in the vineyard of our Lord. Therefore, do not expect God to lower the bar of life's difficulties to make it easier for you to get over. Instead, He will leave that bar in-place, because He wants you to become strong enough to handle your current situation, *and even more.*

I was a decathlete in college, and as part of daily regimen, I spent four-hours between the track and the gym. Each day I pushed myself to the point of complete physical exhaustion both in running and in weight-lifting. For years I endured this tortuous daily training regimen, not to *break* myself, but to *make* myself. My excessive sprinting exercises were not a tool to defeat me, but a method to make me faster. With each thump of my heart or throb of my legs, a single thought filled my mind: "If I can just endure this a little while longer, I will be *faster* because of it." Likewise, my extreme weight-lifting program was not intended to hurt me, but to strengthen me. As I lifted weights, only one idea pushed me to lift the weight again and again: "If I can lift this just once more, I will be *stronger* for it." My training goal was not to *harm myself* during practices, but to *help myself succeed* in the competition.

Likewise, God has not subjected you to the heavy load of your trials to harm you. He has done so to make you a stronger, fitter Christian who can *overcome* in life. Unexercised muscles never grow stronger. So, think of your trial as the exercise and resistance you *need* to become spiritually stronger, and this book as your coach to help you accomplish that end. My training was never easy. Yours might become difficult, too. However, *if you stick with the program*, then by the end you will find that you are a stronger and wiser person for having gone through your junk. Your trials are nothing more than God's call to become a better-equipped follower of Jesus Christ, and the training found in Section Two of this book will help you accomplish this.

The *secret ingredient* to my decathlon training, however, was my *motivation*: I did it all for Jesus. I learned the importance of having the right motivation from Olympic decathlete Dave Johnson's book *Aim High* (co-written with Verne Becker). After three years of being a dud-decathlete in college, I read this book and decided to follow Dave's advice. During my final year of college, instead of running for personal glory, I chose to run to bring *God* glory. Every time I stepped onto a track for training or competition, I prayed, "Lord, whether I run fast, or trip and fall—I'm running for Jesus." This motivational change alone was responsible for vaulting me towards the upper levels of my sport, enabling me to compete at the NCAA National Championships.

However, this is not just a sports principle; it is a *life* principle. If you will embrace this motivational focus, then God will vault *you* to the top level of *your life*. You don't have to barely scrape-by because of your trials any longer. Instead, you can choose to go through your trials for the glory of God, and you will find yourself *overcoming* those trials. If this sounds good, then I invite you to *read on*! By God's grace you will endure your training, you will overcome your trials, and you will become *better for life*!

Discussion Questions

1. What events have you experienced which led you to wonder, "Why isn't life fair?"

2. Does life always turn-out well for all Christians? Does God guarantee that it will? Explain.

3. In the Bible story of Cain and Able, which of the two brothers do you most relate with? Why?

4. If there were one word/name which others have used to characterized you (just as Abel was characterized as "worthless") what would that word be?

5. Is being different than those around you a negative attribute in the world's eyes? How about in God's eyes? Explain.

6. How did Abel's strained family relations contribute to his deepened connection with God?

7. What was God's reaction to Abel being mistreated by his family?

8. What is the "habit which God can't kick"? Explain.

9. What is *your* necessary part, if you are to be promoted by the Lord?

10. What is awaiting those who patiently endure their trials on earth? What does God expect of us while we are going through our trials?

11. How will God reward those who perish before they receive a reward on earth?

12. In light of the physical training mentioned in this chapter, how should a Christian view their trials? What is the "secret ingredient" to our Christian training?

SECTION TWO

How to Become Better for Life

8

Remember and Refocus

How to Trust Again

(Jeremiah 29:11)

Prosperity is a great teacher; adversity a greater.

—William Hazlitt

GOD WORKS. IT'S TRUE. He rolls-up His imaginary sleeves and ap-plies Himself to produce beautiful things. He didn't quit working after He finished the creation sequence. In fact, He is working *right now*. He may not be exercising Himself in the creation of new worlds, but He *is* working to produce something else just as beautiful. At this moment His efforts are focused on making *your* life a *gloriously wonderful success* (see John 15:1–2).

Your circumstances probably conceal this truth, however. Mine sure do. Ancient Israel's circumstances once concealed this truth for them, also. They were God's people living in a difficult time. Just like for many of us today, life for them was more of a burden than a joy. Unlike today, their problems were not rooted in a struggling economy, however. Instead, their problems were because the bloodthirsty Babylonian King Nebuchadnezzar had conquered their nation. A few years later, the same king returned to destroy the temple and enslave many Israelites, bring-ing them to another land. Needless to say, their predicament was *far worse* than yours or mine.

Truth be told, it was completely their fault. They refused to fol-low God's leading, which would have kept them from such calamity.

However, through it all, God still gave them hope by simply stating His intentions: "For I know the thoughts that I think toward you, says the LORD, thoughts of peace and not of evil, to give you a future and a hope" (Jeremiah 29:11, NKJV). Another translation of this text explains that God's plans are "not to harm you" (Jeremiah 29:11, NIV). During the worst part of my personal tribulations, I began to wonder if God's point *was* to harm me. Sometimes it sure seemed like it! Then, like a healing ointment, God applied this verse to my heart, and I understood that the Lord was not to blame. It was only at that moment when I truly realized that God's plans do *not* include harming me. And I want to affirm to you that *God has no intentions of harming you*, either. It does not matter what you have done wrong in finances or in life; *God truly does want the best for you*. He even tells of His plans for your hopeful future!

If we are not convinced we can trust God, then we will run away from Him, which is the last thing any of us need right now. Sometimes our difficulties can bring us to a point of doubting God's intended goodness, which is a dangerous thing. We can begin thinking that God enjoys watching us humans squirm under the strain of trials, which is not the truth. A person's intentions drive their actions, and it is the same with the Lord. So, if we believe God's intentions are intended to be painful, then we will not trust Him. However, if we can just realize and accept that He has *good* intentions for us, then it will become *natural* to trust Him, even if we still encounter pain. Moreover, by accepting the goodness of His intentions for each of us, we can be strengthened to go through the remainder of our trials.

Look, if everything was strictly up to the Lord, He would accomplish His master plan for your life, without difficulties and without trials. You would bloom abundantly in a fertile garden of life, without suffering or loss. Man's reality would be a joyful unending existence of walking closely with the Lord in the lush abundance of His love and provision. This is exactly how He fashioned man's first home, the Garden of Eden. Although God did not intend *the Fall*, it still happened. The first humans became contaminated by evil, and so did their home of planet earth. Now we are left to live with the consequences. My point is this: *life's difficulty is not God's fault*. God never intended for you to suffer evil. But since evil is already here, and we must live with it, God encourages us through it.

A few months ago my five-year-old son Jonathan fell off a swing from high in the air. He picked-up himself off the ground screaming from pain. And as I carefully removed his jacket I understood why—his right arm had a 30-degree bend where it was supposed to be straight. He broke it in three places. As a parent, it crushed my heart to hold my precious boy's deformed and limp arm as we rushed to the emergency room.

As frightening as this was for his mother and me, it was even more traumatic for Jonathan. He became hysterical every time he looked at his arm. So, instead, he fixed his eyes on *me*. Even as he screamed with pain each time the doctors or nurses touched his arm, his tear-filled eyes stayed glued to mine. *He trusted me.* Until then he knew nothing of broken bones. He did not know who the doctors were, or what they were doing to his arm. At that instant, he only understood two things: 1) *I hurt*, and 2) *But I know I can trust my daddy.* As long as I was by his side and holding his little hand, he could submit to the doctors' treatment, as painful as it was. And this is exactly what he needed. He amazed me with his courage that day.

In his painful experience Jonathan understood *two* things. But in many of *our* painful experiences, we often only know *one*, which is: *I hurt*. Just like my son, maybe you don't understand the pain which you now face. When in an agonizing and turbulent situation, it is difficult to know what went wrong. Neither do we know who we can trust. We have found ourselves in trouble, but we have not yet realized that there is Someone who will hold our hand through it. Scared, we don't know where to turn. Friend, *turn to your Heavenly Father.*

Jonathan knew he could trust me, even though the pain was excruciating. Your pain may be just as agonizing. However, if you can accept the fact that you can trust the Lord, then He will help you *through* your pain, also. God is both our Comforter and our Healer; there is nowhere better for us to look for help. We may not understand it, but if we will do like Jonathan and *refocus* our eyes on our Heavenly Father, then we will find strength to get through our tough times.

In addition to *refocusing* on the Lord, it is also important for each of us to *remember* His personal promises to us. You see, I believe God has already given you the blueprint for your life in some form or fashion. He has already revealed to each of us a special hope for our futures. It is that hope which keeps us moving forward in our journey with Christ Jesus.

During His earthly life, Jesus knew that people usually needed a reason to follow Him as their Rabbi/Teacher—they needed some sort of *future expectation*. You might call this a "carrot on the end of the discipleship stick," or you can simply call this "business as usual." But regardless of our perceptions, God understands that having a future expectation is normal, even wise. Only a fool takes a journey with no destination in mind. And only a bigger fool blindly follows! So, Jesus frequently offered each disciple-candidate something personal which they could relate to . . . something which was meaningful *to them*, even if to no one else. He gave them something they could really *get*.

For example, once a rich young ruler approached Jesus and related his desire to have everlasting life. The Bible says this young man had great wealth, so he probably understood sound investment principles, and was clearly keen with his finances. After all, even if he inherited the money, it would still take financial savvy to keep it. This young man was obviously consumed with his treasures, but he wanted more than just a piece of earth to call his own; he wanted a piece of *heaven*. So Jesus used this young man's terms to tender an offer which he could *understand*. Jesus offered him the chance to invest on earth and somehow net a return of "treasure in heaven" (Luke 18:22, NKJV). This promising young man did not capitalize on Jesus' investment opportunity, choosing rather to reject the proposal and depart with great sadness. Nevertheless, He deeply understood Jesus' offer and call to discipleship.

To the two fishermen brothers, Peter and James, Jesus presented a totally different offer. "Treasure in heaven" would have meant little to non-stockholding fishermen (Luke 18:22, NKJV). In order for *them* to truly understand what it meant to be Jesus' disciple, they needed an offer better-suited to them. They needed one dressed in "fishermen-ease." Again Jesus obliged. While fishing with Jesus one day, the brothers caught the *greatest catch of their lives!* There were so many fish that their net was breaking and their boat began to *sink* (see Luke 5:6–7). Jesus seized the opportunity to present their tailored offer: "Do not be afraid. From now on you will catch *men*" (Luke 5:10, NKJV, emphasis added). The thought of "fishing for men" would have been an insult to the rich young ruler, and today it means little to most of us. However, it meant *the world* to this pair of fishermen. They knew *exactly* what Jesus was talking about. They understood that Jesus was not talking about "catching" a couple folks here or there with the "net of the Gospel"; they knew

Jesus was talking about catching *boatloads* of people for God. Precisely this was accomplished on at least two occasions when Peter preached and *thousands* responded in faith (see Acts 2:40–41, and 4:4). He caught *men* with the same measure that he caught *fish* on the day Jesus revealed his future.

My point is this: *God speaks your language.* Regardless of your hobbies or habits, station or occupation, God knows how to make you understand what good plans He has for you. And somewhere in the annals of your memory is a vivid recollection of the moment the Lord Jesus Christ called you to a disciple's life. At that time, possibly even years ago, He spoke to you in *your own language* and He gave you a promise. He powerfully communicated something of your future directly to you, and the thought of this message *still* brings tears to your eyes. This is your God-given dream. This is your *hope* on this side of heaven. This message is what the Lord will accomplish in your life, if only you are willing. It is not too late. You are not too far away. Moses was eighty-years old and living on the backside of the desert when God called him, then God used him for another *forty years!* (see Deuteronomy 29:5 and 31:2). As long as you still have breath, God can still make your dream happen. He is only waiting on your consent.

Remember, your hope is individually tailored for no one but *you.* Nobody else on the planet has your same plan or promise. And they wouldn't understand why *you* think *your* plan is so awesome, anyway. Then again, neither would *you* understand why *they* believe *their* plan is so great, either. Nevertheless, each person has a *right* to think their plan is the best, because *it is* the best plan . . . *for them.* The fact is, God does not assign a "plan-B" to anybody who is willing to follow Jesus Christ. Only those who refuse to follow Jesus (like the rich young ruler) are relegated to live-out the plan-B for their life.

The good news about this is you can start *right now!* If you are anything like me, then you regret having wasted years living your own way. You wish you could go back and re-live your earlier years God's way. Yet no matter how much we wish or how hard we pray, none of us can rewind life. God knows this. So, if this describes you, then today is a very good day for you. Today the Lord is offering you His absolute best plan-A for the rest of your life. If you'll simply choose to follow Jesus, He will do all the rest.

It is important that we *rehearse* the Lord's promises to us. At some point we all have forgotten our wallet or purse or car keys. If we are not careful we can also forget the promise which God has communicated to us. These memories can easily be drowned-out equally well by a successful career or troubled times. However, if we will only make an effort to remember these things, they will surface again. We know this because God also ensures that His communications to us are also *memorable*.

All of us remember where we were when we learned of the twin towers' collapsed on 9/11. You can also clearly recall the happiest moments of your life, like your marriage proposal or the birth of a child. In the same way, there is a link in your brain which, when activated, transmits to your mind a clear and instantaneous recollection of God's word to you. With just a little thought, you can remember the plan-A which God spoke to you, even if it was decades earlier.

One of my own personal promises happened during my senior year of college. I was a Christian at-heart, but I had not attended church in years. My mother had convinced me to bring a Bible with me to college that year (for the first time), and each week I would sit alone on a bench and try to hear God speaking to me as I read from it. I knew I wanted God to have a greater place in my life, but I was struggling to figure-out how. I just wanted whatever God wanted for me. It was in this context when a Christian classmate learned I was a "closet-believer." We had a brief talk about Jesus one night, and I assumed that to be the end of our discussion.

However, the next day he saw me waiting for class, and he approached me. He told me he had a dream about me that night. Not knowing what else to say I shrugged it off with a self-defacing "I'm sorry to hear that." He replied, "No- it was a *good* dream." His eyes opened wide: "I dreamed you were *an evangelist*." The hair stood-up on my arms and neck. My heart raced for joy, and my immediate thought was, "Wow—that would be *awesome!*" I knew God wanted me to hear those words. I *needed* to hear those words. Through them, God had revealed my future. Although I had no understanding of how to get there, since then God has been strategically closing some doors and opening others to lead me into my destiny.

So what is *your* story? I know you have one . . . every disciple of Christ does. Your story is just as exciting as mine! The Lord has put something in your heart to do, because He has created you, saved you, and called you for *that special purpose.* Your plan is a tailor-made plan-A for *your* life, and the Lord has plans to fulfill it! It is so crucial that we each remember these plans and promises that God hard-wired them into our brains! However, in time our mind can become clouded with the many other responsibilities *of* life and possibilities *in* life. So we need to carefully identify *God's* plans for us and then hold-on with all of our might. If we do this, then we are well on our way to seeing God accomplish the great things which He has designed for us.

Still, just because we *understand* our promise does not mean that all of the necessary doors will swing wide-open, freeing us to immediately fulfill our destiny. Oftentimes difficulties are *part of the process* of getting there. Remember, these are *life-plans* which God has laid-out for your entire earthly life. The point is, if you hustled to accomplish your entire life-plan by the end of this year, you would be left with *nothing else to do.* God might have to take you home to heaven *early*! You see, it is not about doing everything *immediately.* It is about doing everything *eventually.* You've got a lifetime of important things to accomplish. Don't get in rush thinking it has all got to be done in a single day, or even a single *decade.* In agricultural terms, a seed requires time to mature and grow in order to fulfill its mission. A carrot seed takes time to produce a carrot, and a flower seed takes time to produce a flower. In the same way, God's word is a seed deposited into our lives, which requires time to produce *a future.*

It is easy to become anxious as we wait for our future to spring-up. Therefore, we would be wise to consider that *dirt contains no plan or power.* The *soil* makes absolutely *no effort* to grow a seed. Instead, it simply acts as an incubator for that seed. Meanwhile, the seed has an intricate *plan* for reproduction, and the *power* needed to accomplish that plan. It only needs an "office space" of sorts to make it happen. In other words, the plan and the power are in *the seed*, not the soil. The seed pushes and stretches until it breaks out of its shell and finally grows into a full plant. Remember, this seed is relentless! *It will not quit* until its plan is completely realized. But make no mistake; it is *the seed* that is doing all the work. The soil merely makes itself available, nothing more. It doesn't strive or strain. And neither should you.

You see, it is *not our job* to strive or strain. Our job is to simply hold onto the seed-promise of God, and let that seed do the *real* work of producing our future. The seed contains God's *plan* for our lives, and it contains the *power* to accomplish that plan. We bring neither of these to the table, so we must trust God's seed. We can no more hurry-up our future, than we can hurry-up a growing oak. But if we wait patiently, then before we know it, our future will have sprung-up right before our eyes!

Remember what God has spoken to you, and consider that the fulfillment of your destiny it is integral to the Christian mandate. Jesus called us to *make disciples* of all nations, and *you are needed* to make this happen (Matthew 28:18–20). Maybe your problems have merely been God's way of positioning you for your greatest usefulness and ultimate success in this task. God's seed planted in your heart has been working toward the fulfillment of this destiny, and your Christian life is *proof* of the inherent power of God's seed in you. It has affected your relationships for the best. It has changed your views of work and money for the best. And it has resulted in your decision to serve others instead of serving only yourself—also for the best. Now do you see the strength of God's Word? It does more than merely change your mind—it changes your entire *life*. This stuff is *powerful*! With this amount of raw and uninhibited power, you should never doubt the ultimate fulfillment of your destiny again!

Look, you don't have to fix your problems in life—you only have to cooperate with God as *He* fixes them. *Remember* God's word to you. Keep it tucked away in an honest and good heart, and trust the Lord to bring it to pass. The powerful seed is working to arrange all the aspects of your life to maximize your usefulness in God's kingdom. God has a plan for you. That plan is contained in the seed of His word to you, and that seed will *get the job done*! It will *ensure* you are in the right place at the right time and with the right preparations. Your road may not be an easy one to hoe, and you will be tried and tested. Still, the seed of God's word in your life has *more than enough* power to get the job done. In the end that tiny seed *will* prevail. *And so will you.*

Discussion Questions

1. Have your difficult times ever prompted you to wonder if God has plans to harm you? What have you learned about this from this chapter? Explain.

2. From the emergency room story, what are the two things we must do to get through our pain?

3. What practical steps can you take to *refocus* on the Lord during your trial?

4. What practical steps can you take to *remember* God's personal promise to you?

5. At the beginning of your Christian walk, God communicated to you something of your future *hope*. Describe this event, and why it was so meaningful.

6. How can you be guaranteed to have the "plan-A" for your life? Is it ever too late to begin?

7. How long can you expect your life-plans to take? Explain.

8. What contains the *plan* and *power* to accomplish your life-plan? What is your role in making this happen?

9. What are the chances of your future plan coming to pass? Explain.

9

Don't Be Offended

How to Turn Rocky Ground into Good Soil

(MARK 4:1–20)

God be thanked that there are some in the world
to whose hearts the barnacles will not cling.

—JOSIAH GILBERT HOLLAND

"JUST GIVE IT A couple weeks and you'll get over it . . . guaranteed," everybody told me. I must have heard this a hundred times during my time onboard ships. But I never did "get over it," and I still can't hold-down my cookies while at sea. It almost doesn't make sense how I got involved in a sailing career when I have this issue. My only answer is that more experienced sailors promised I would *get over it*. I just never did.

On one voyage, my merchant vessel began to feel the effects of a hurricane hundreds of miles away. As the ocean swells grew, my toler-ance-level shrunk. After a full day of being on-edge I just couldn't take it anymore. I was either going to lose my lunch or lose my *religion*! It was at just that moment when I conveniently remembered the story of Jesus calming the storm. I immediately connected this with Jesus' promise: ". . . if you have faith and do not doubt . . . you [will] say to this mountain, 'Be removed and be cast into the sea,' [and] it will be done" (Matthew 21:21, NKJV). The growing ocean swells were beginning to look like mountains, so I figured it was time to exercise this promise.

Gathering all the faith I could muster, I focused it like a "laser-beam" to put an end to this mountainous problem before me. Then (and

I am almost ashamed to tell you) . . . I did it. I raised my hands like Charlton Heston in The Ten Commandments movie, and with my most authoritative voice I commanded the storm to cease and ordered the ocean waves to lay flat. If anybody else had seen this performance, I would have gotten a *special* trip home, I think. I might have been committed! But in my moment of misery, *I didn't care!* This storm *had* to stop, and *I* had to be the one to stop it. I prayed that the storm would end. I trusted God and believed with all my heart that it would end. I even closed my eyes really tight to *give God a chance* to make it end. Then I opened my eyes and . . . the storm *did not* end. For two more days I was a member of the "T-N-T club," as I heaved into every trash can and toilet I met, until the swells finally subsided. Through those two days I was consumed with wondering what went wrong. Did I have a problem with my *faith*, my *heart*, or just my *inner ear*?

Although there is no spiritual test for one's inner ear, Jesus did give a method to test the spiritual condition of our *hearts*. He did this through a parable which equated people's hearts to different types of soils. In this *parable of the soils*, good seed was dropped into four soils of various conditions. Some seeds died and produced nothing, while other seeds produced an abundance of good fruit. The Lord used this parable to explain that the spiritual condition of our hearts *will affect* the spiritual outcome of our lives:

> Listen! Behold, a sower went out to sow. And it happened, as he sowed, *that* some *seed* fell by the wayside; and the birds of the air came and devoured it. Some fell on stony ground, where it did not have much earth; and immediately it sprang up because it had no depth of earth. But when the sun was up it was scorched, and because it had no root it withered away. And some *seed* fell among thorns; and the thorns grew up and choked it, and it yielded no crop. But other *seed* fell on good ground and yielded a crop that sprang up, increased and produced: some thirtyfold, some sixty, and some a hundred . . . He who has ears to hear, let him hear! (Mark 4:3–9, NKJV)

As Christians, we expect our heart to be "good soil" where all the good things which God has planned for our lives can blossom. Yet in order to make this happen, we must ensure that the soil of our heart is in good condition. As we deal with trials and tribulations, however, there is one soil-type which is especially applicable: the *stony* soil. With this in mind, we will focus on this one particular soil-type, and learn what we can from it.

Jesus explained the connection between the rocky soil and the rocky-soil *believer*: "The sower soweth the word. . . . And these are they likewise which are sown on stony ground; who, when they have heard the word, immediately receive it with gladness; and have no root in themselves, and so endure for a time: afterward, when affliction or persecution ariseth for the word's sake, immediately they are *offended*" (Mark 4:14, and 16–17, KJV, emphasis added).

In a moment we will take a closer look at what it means to be *offended*. But first, imagine if you will, one solitary little sprout planted in the hard, dry, arid desert soil. It has no other plants or trees around to provide shade, and there is no nearby water-source. After a cool and refreshing night the sun slowly peeks over the horizon. It rises high and higher in the sky. Meanwhile the delicate little plant's internal temperature rises from the cool night temperature to the hot ambient daytime temperature. As the sun approaches its zenith the plant braces for the most trying time of its day. At this point, if our little plant could speak, we might hear her say, "Ouch . . . this hurts! I'm alone, and I'm exposed! It is hurting more and more. Doesn't anybody care? Now it hurts too much! *I can't take this much longer!* . . ." However, just before the plant's tender little leaves begin to wither under the heat; the sun descends and finally falls out of sight. This will allow the plant to once again begin its cooling process through the night. Then, the cycle will repeat itself the next morning when the sun again peaks over the dry terrain.

This cycle is carried-out day after day in the lives of plants. In addition, it is carried-out time after time in the lives of us humans, as well. The Lord provides for us through times of abundance. He does this through a good job or a booming economy. However, after this refreshing time of abundance, our own trials and tribulations peek over the horizon of our lives, and *life gets tough*. These difficulties incrementally increase until they are directly overhead, beating-down on us, and leaving us nowhere to find the shade of relief and safety. At the crescendo of our problems we might make the same plea as our little plant in the hot, dry ground; "It's starting to hurt . . . it's getting pretty bad now . . . I can't take this any longer . . . *doesn't anybody care?*" Maybe you're there right now. When we are in the hottest part of our trials and tribulations, it can feel like we are being *permanently scorched*, just like our solitary little plant in the desert.

At this point, I have a simple question: why doesn't God just block the heat of the sun to *help* our little plant? After all, if there were trees surrounding it, then it would not be forced to bear the brunt of direct sunlight for so long. Even a slight amount of shade would make the unbearable daytime hours a little more tolerable, and possibly even make the plant live longer. And in way of application, why doesn't God shade *us* from our problems—or better yet—why doesn't He just make them *stop*?

In essence, this was my hope and intent when I raised my hands to the ocean and commanded the storm to end. Maybe *you* have prayed something similar lately. You probably did not raise your arms and try to bellow like Charlton Heston, but you made a similar heartfelt plea asking God to make your problems end. You might have even closed your eyes tight to help focus your faith to accomplish your desire. But when you opened them again . . . the problems were still there. This made you feel betrayed, and without hope. I think many of us have been there.

Well, the truth is that God could snap His fingers and make life easier for each of us. He could command His angels to "bear you up, lest you dash your foot against a stone" in life (Matthew 4:6, NKJV). However, if He did shield us from every problem and trial, He would not be doing us any favors. In fact, this would not really be a "help" at all, because we would never learn the lessons the Lord wants us to learn. Even further, we would never grow into the mighty man or woman of God which He intends for each of us to grow into. You see, the answer to our question is the reason for this book: God allows you to go through trials in life *to make you better able* to live the life which God wants you to live. Let me explain.

From Jesus' parable, the sun is clearly a *threat* to the plant. However, it is also the plant's *only hope of growth*. By the process of photosynthesis the plant uses the sunlight to convert the water- and soil-bound elements into nutritional sugars for the plant. This process literally *creates food* for the plant. However, without the energy from the hot sunlight, photosynthesis would not occur. In other words, without the sun beating down upon it, the plant would never *grow*. It would only wither and eventually die.

Likewise, without the uncomfortable heat of *our* personal difficulties we would never come to faith, or grow in it. Trials motivate us to *seek* the Lord. Many people come to faith as a result of personal trials. Wisely, they realize their issues are too big to handle alone, and they accept the fact that Jesus *wants* to help them. So they reach-out to Him. In addition, trials also stimulate us to *grow* in the Lord. In a Christian's life, difficulties help us convert God's latent truths into useful life principles and direction. Scriptures which have meant little to us for years instantly become life-giving and hope-inspiring when difficulties arise. So, in effect, God does not block the heat of our tribulations, because *this exposure promotes our spiritual life and growth.* As uncomfortable as it sounds, we *need* difficulties to grow to maturity.

Of course there is a balance to this process. In nature *too much* sun will scorch and kill the plant. Meanwhile not enough sunlight will hinder the plant's growth. Therefore, the attentive gardener takes responsibility to ensure this balance is properly maintained. It is the *gardener*, not the plant, who determines the right amount of sunlight to ensure optimal plant growth. Likewise, in our lives, it is not *our* duty to determine the right proportion of trials and tribulations we should receive—this is the duty of *our Gardener*, God Himself (John 15:1–2). *Our* duty is to simply trust our Gardener, and grow through whatever good or bad times come our way. Nothing more and nothing less.

However, just as the physical sun sets, giving much-needed relief to the plant, our problems will also fall out of sight to give us rest from *our* trials. Your difficulties cannot last forever, so don't be discouraged by thinking they will. In nature, the sun is only visible for about half of each 24-hour cycle, and the most intense sunlight only occurs for an even shorter amount of time. Likewise, your trials will only be overhead for a brief time. And in a single moment God will make them stop, and you will rest, just like our little plant.

In Colorado there is a baseball field dubbed "Rocky Field." But the *Colorado Rockies* Major League Baseball team does not play there. *I* played there . . . in high school. My small-town mountain high school hardly had enough players to field a full baseball team, and did not warrant a cultivated home field. So we made-do with the community baseball field, which was overlaid not with grass, but with *rocks*; hence its name. Believe me, this was *not* a fun place to make a diving catch or slide into second. Playing baseball at Rocky Field was *painful.* Several times each season we players would spend practice time *de-rocking* the field. We would systematically spread out and walk the field, searching for stones, and upon finding them we would pitch them over the fence. The funny thing was, no matter how thorough we were, the results were always the same. Within a week, *new* rocks would replace the *old* ones. That field seemed to *grow rocks*! However, it is not only my high school baseball field which seems to grow rocks—our hearts do, also.

According to Greek scholar Joseph H. Thayer, the word translated as "offended" (Mark 4:17, KJV) means "*to be offended in one*, i.e. to see in another what I disapprove of and what hinders me from acknowledging his authority."[6] In other words, we become offended when *we determine what God should be doing for us* and then *judge God* based on those expectations, instead of simply accepting whatever He allows. Stated more pointedly, offense only happens when *we act as God's judge*. And when He does not measure-up to our expectations and we become offended, we reject His authority in our lives. For example, when we are completely convinced that God will not let us lose our job, we become offended when we become jobless. When we truly expect God to heal our disease at the stadium-sized healing service, but leave in worse shape than we arrived, we become offended. "This Christianity stuff does not work" we complain, as our heart breaks from unfulfilled expectations.

According to Jesus' parable, an *offense* is equated with a rock, or a stone. Therefore, an *offense* (or, a *stone*) develops with every improper response to our trials and tribulations. As a memory aide, a stone can be considered: *Something-That-Opposes-Normal-Expectations* (S-T-O-N-E). You see, God gives us His genuine promises with a guarantee to fulfill each one *in the proper time*. These are *normal expectations*. We expect God to provide us with food, because He has promised to (Matthew 6:25–26, and 31–32). And He does. We expect God to provide us with clothing, because He has so promised (Matthew 6:27–32). He does this, also. However, sometimes we can generate *our own* positive idea, and *assume* it is a promise from the Lord. We might even spiritualize our phony promise by attaching a Bible verse to it; but it is *still* not a promise from God. It is a *counterfeit* promise, and God has no intentions of fulfilling it. It opposes normal expectations, which makes it a *stone* (something-that-opposes-normal-expectations) in our spiritual lives.

It is easy to produce these *stones*, and we all do so from time to time. However, it is vital that we *find* and *uproot* these stones in our hearts because they are so very *dangerous*. For example, in my personal Moses-episode, I forged God's name to the counterfeit promise that my storm would immediately end. When God did not honor this phony promise *I became offended*. Herein lies the danger. Each stone is an offense waiting to happen. After enough offenses, we are bound to simply walk away from following the Lord, thinking He is not trustworthy to fulfill His promises. But the truth is God *does* fulfill His promises . . . the *real* ones, at least.

In my Moses-flashback I did not understand that the Lord *had* fulfilled His promise to me: *He was with me* through my storm so I would not despair. I heaved much more than I would have liked, but the Lord was *faithful* to bring me safely through *that* storm and many others. Where did I get the idea that I was entitled to have smooth sailing at sea? Obviously it did not come from God, otherwise the storm *would have* ended (and I would have been nicknamed "Moses" for the rest of my shipping career).

Please don't make the mistake of thinking you are immune to this potential problem of offensive stones in your heart. We *all* are vulnerable to this danger, and we all need to keep the field of our hearts cleared-out, so we can live-out a successful Christian life. Even Jesus Himself recognized the danger of these stones in *His own* life. One day, the Lord Jesus told the disciples of the master plan for His life—to suffer and die, and be raised again. Peter immediately piped-up, "Far be it from You, Lord; this shall not happen to You!"(Matthew 16:22, NKJV). Peter truly wanted the best for His teacher, and he thought Jesus deserved a long and prosperous life. However, the subtle reality was that Peter was trying to *replace* God's will with his own will. Peter's comment was *something that opposed normal expectations.*

Jesus recognized the dangerous *stone* hidden in Peter's words. He knew this statement was intended to divert Him from His life's purpose: to redeem all mankind by His death and resurrection. The Lord quickly resolved that this stone *must not* be left in his heart; otherwise it would lead to His downfall. If the rock were to stay and take root in the Jesus' heart, He knew that He would never make it to Calvary. So He had to throw it out of the field of His heart, and quickly! Jesus shot back, "Get behind Me, Satan! You are an offense to Me, for you are not mindful of the things of God, but the things of men" (Matthew 16:23, NKJV). My point is this: if *the Son of God* had to be extra diligent to ensure He removed even the slightest stone from His heart, *how much more careful should you and I be*?

Whoever convinced us that, as Christians, we are *entitled* to worldly prosperity? It surely wasn't God. And who told us that we *deserve* to live a comfortable life on earth? Again, not God. It is easy to allow our vision to fall from heaven to earth. Or, as Jesus put it, it is easy to become mindful of *the things of men*, instead of *the things of God*. Even the great Apostle Peter fell into this trap! (see Matthew 16:22–23) However, our Lord Jesus foretold us of our true future: "Here on earth you will have many trials and sorrows. But take heart, because I have overcome the world" (John 16:33, NLT). Since we have been forewarned to expect problems, it would be presumptuous for us to expect otherwise.

You see, our real problem is not what we think it is. It is not lack of employment, or even lack of resources. Our *real* problem is the fact that *there are rocks in the soil of our hearts*. We expect to walk on the clouds while still living on the earth, and it just isn't happening. This makes us frustrated and offended at God. Meanwhile, the seed of God's word is trying to grow a grand spiritual plant in our lives with deep tap-roots, but our rocks are stopping it! So, we must stop accusing our ex-employer, the government, or the economy for our problems, and accept the fact that all this time our biggest problem has been *us*. We have not let God be *God*.

You see, the rocks in the field of our hearts are a result of reducing the Lord to being the *genie* of our lives instead of the *Lord* of our lives. We have told God what we expect, and called them "promises" to boot. And as long as we continue treating God as our servant, we will continue to cultivate our personal rock-farms. However, there is good news. With a little effort, we can find these stones and throw them over the fence of our hearts, just like I did at *Rocky Field* in high school. If we are willing, God will teach us *what we should expect* from Him and from life, and He will teach us *how to properly respond* when trials do come our way. By doing this we will rid our hearts of *stones*, and thereby make room for the seed of God's word to grow to its full potential in our lives.

In order to accomplish this, we must first *be honest* with God. In Luke's rendition of this parable, Jesus noted the attributes needed for a person to be a successful Christian: "And the seeds that fell on the good soil represent *honest, good-hearted people* who hear God's word, cling to it, and patiently produce a huge harvest" (Luke 8:15; NLT, emphasis added). An honest and good heart is one which doesn't mix the promises of God with the seductions of mankind. This is a heart which does not twist God's Word for the sake of personal benefit or ease in life. An honest and good heart holds fast to what *God has said*, and dismisses the multitude of other self-serving voices and expectations. We can remove our heart-rocks by acquiring a balanced view of the Christian life—one which includes hardships. The Bible proclaims, "Many *are* the afflictions of the righteous, but the LORD delivers him out of them all" (Psalm 34:19, NKJV).

So, how do we obtain an "honest and good heart" (Luke 8:15)? *Seek the truth without fear.* To recycle a famous President John F. Kennedy quote: "ask not what your Lord can do for you, but what you can do for your Lord." When we read the Bible, we must do so with a patient and humble heart, allowing the Holy Spirit to communicate His form-fitting word to us at the appropriate times in our lives. God will indeed give us promises tailored to fit our personal destinies; however, the Lord must be the *originator* of these promises. Otherwise they are just more stones to be tossed.

Please realize, just as God ordained the sun, He also allows tribulations into each of our lives. These difficulties are for our growth, whether we like it or not. Although we can't change this fact, we can *choose to patiently persist* through our troubles with an *honest and good heart.* It will take some heart-searching to remove the counterfeit promises which have already caused us to become offended, and those which pose future threats. And when we find these *somethings-that-oppose-normal-expectations*, toss them out of our hearts. There's no reason to wait—let's commit to uproot them immediately and with reckless abandon, just like Jesus did. This will be difficult, but with God's help we can do it.

An Old Testament prophet of God proclaimed, "Blessed *is* the man who trusts in the LORD, and whose hope is the LORD. For he shall be like a tree planted by the waters, which spreads out its roots by the river, and will not fear when heat comes [i.e., difficulties happen]; but its leaf will be green, and will not be anxious in the year of drought [i.e., with little provision], nor will cease from yielding fruit" (Jeremiah 17:7–8, NKJV). Jeremiah was saying, if we trust in the Lord, the roots of our life will grow wide and deep near the river of God (which never runs dry). The sun rises overhead each day, and likewise, we can likewise expect the coming and going of trials and tribulations in life. However, when these problems do come, we will not fear. Even in the *year of drought*, when the river of abundance no longer runs, our deep spiritual roots will sustain us, and we will never stop producing good fruit.

We cannot completely avoid difficulties, but we can live *above* them, if only we will trust in the Lord. Moreover, we will find that it is possible to endure our trials without offense. The great thing is, Jesus guaranteed that if you do this, you will ultimately "produce a huge harvest" spiritually (Luke 8:15, NLT). You may not become the nation's next president or win the Nobel Peace Prize, but you will be called *great* in the sight of God. And there is *nothing* better than that.

Discussion Questions

1. Have you ever attempted something similar to the Charlton Heston-moment the writer described? Were you "successful" at it? How did the results make you feel?

2. Were you able to connect with the little plant's experience in this chapter? Why or why not?

3. Have you ever wondered why God doesn't make you trials stop? What did you believe the reason was prior to reading this chapter? Has this chapter convinced you otherwise? Explain.

4. Why exactly does God allow His children to go through "junk" in life?

5. What is the *danger* and what is the *benefit* of the sun in a plant's life? What is the *danger* and what is the *benefit* of troubles in the believer's life?

6. Are difficulties in life needed? Why or why not?

7. Who is responsible to ensure that each believer receives the appropriate amount of troubles in life?

8. Have you ever felt offended at God? Why?

9. What is our *real* problem and why? What does S-T-O-N-E represent in the Christian's life?

10. What practical things can you do to help identify *stones* in your heart and remove them? Why is this important?

11. Are there any Christians who no longer need to worry about stones in their heart? Explain.

10

Don't Stop Giving

How to Be a Neighbor

(LUKE 10:25–37)

*Do not wait for extraordinary circumstances to do good actions;
try to use ordinary situations.*

—JEAN PAUL RICHTER

I THINK I'VE HEARD enough *I'll pray for you's* to last a lifetime. Don't get me wrong, prayer is good and essential, and I am thankful for everyone who has offered a prayer to God on behalf of me and my family. But when we are struggling, from time to time we need something more than just a prayer—we need *help!* At the right moment, a couple bags of groceries would strengthen our faith even more than it would strengthen our bodies. If you are in a similar situation, then you know what I am talking about. Even the slightest bit of tangible help would make you feel cared for and loved. However, these days there are so few people who *can* help, and even fewer who are willing.

From the very beginning, man has been out for good-ole number one: *himself.* The serpent in the Garden of Eden tempted Eve to try to obtain more than her lot in life with: if you eat this, then "you will be like God" (Genesis 3:5, NKJV). The first couple took the bait and was sentenced to death because of their self-seeking actions. Their oldest son, Cain, did the same when he murdered his little brother in an attempt to advance his own spiritual standing by one notch. This trend continues even today. It happens in politics and in business alike. It even happens in the home. Most people are out for themselves, and even more so in today's difficult financial landscape. Moreover, because people have tightened their spending, less money is being given charitably to those who are hurting the worst.

Back when affluence was the order of the day, most people could afford to give some money to charities. Some Christians gave 10 percent of their income to the local church, while a few would make it a point to go beyond this level, even giving to other charitable organizations. However, all of this has changed, and many of us now feel that we can't afford to give at all. Meanwhile, there is more need *now* than when giving was easy. Today we have less to give, while the needs are much greater. This leaves us in a difficult position of deciding how to use the reduced resources which we still *do* have. After all, how can we give to someone else when our own bills are barely covered?

Since we each retain control of own pocketbooks, most of us pay ourselves first, and are hardly sad when we find there is nothing left-over to give away. This can be found on a personal basis, as well as at the corporate level. In the news media, stories abound of CEO's who cut their workforce rather than cutting their own seven-digit bonuses. Just before Christmas 2008, when the economy was near its lowest, one prominent company cut about 1,500 jobs, then turned right around to post *record gains.* Imagine: this long-standing company sacrificed 1,500 jobs (resulting in 1,500 homes devastated), not just to keep the company afloat through the recession, but to gain their greatest profits *ever* through it. Greed is just as prevalent in a bad economy as it is in a booming economy.

It is the exceptionally few leaders who truly have in-mind the best interest of their people (and thereby, their company). These are a rare breed, yet they are extremely easy to find. They are the ones who cut their own pay during tough times, in order to retain the good workers who are the backbone of the company. It takes a very special leader to sacrifice themselves for the good of others. These are the people who I want to lead my company, my country, and my church. Sadly, however, they are few and *very* far between.

Likewise, it is the exception to find an individual who cuts their own expenses to help someone else. When we are employed, we find ways to spend our discretionary money on the newest products and hottest trends, without helping others with their basic needs. Not until we lose our job do we realize how much money we wasted and, in turn, how much help we refused others. Most often, we are not wise enough to help others, until we are unable to help *ourselves*. We don't *see* the need until we *have* the need.

However, regardless of how bad life is treating you or me, there is *always* somebody worse-off. It is relatively easy to find these people, too. We don't have to go to the food banks or homeless shelters to find them. All we have to do is look at our own circle of friends, neighbors, and ex-coworkers (the ones who lost their jobs before we did). Our heart goes out to them in all sincerity, and we really wish there was something we could do. But two unavoidable truths typically keep us from action: 1) we have so little extra ourselves that we can't imagine it would be much help; and 2) the needs are so overwhelming that we don't know where to start. However, the Lord Jesus knew every one of us would face this dilemma, so He answered both of these concerns two thousand years ago.

> Then Jesus answered and said: "A certain *man* went down from Jerusalem to Jericho, and fell among thieves, who stripped him of his clothing, wounded *him*, and departed, leaving *him* half dead. Now by chance a certain priest came down that road. And when he saw him, he passed by on the other side. Likewise a Levite, when he arrived at the place, came and looked, and passed by on the other side. But a certain Samaritan, as he journeyed, came where he was. And when he saw him, he had compassion. So he went to *him* and bandaged his wounds, pouring on oil and wine; and he set him on his own animal, brought him to an inn, and took care of him. On the next day, when he departed, he took out two denarii, gave *them* to the innkeeper, and said to him, 'Take care of him; and whatever more you spend, when I come again, I will repay you.' So which of these three do you think was neighbor to him who fell among the thieves?" And he said, "He who showed mercy on him." Then Jesus said to him, "God and do likewise" (Luke 10:30–37, NKJV).

Notice that of the three passers-by (the priest, the Levite, and the Samaritan) none went *looking* for someone in need. They didn't have to look; in each case their life-journey led them directly to a distressed individual. Likewise, you don't have to go looking for people to help. As you walk along your own personal road of life, God will place them right in your path. In fact, I would even go so far as to state that God *intentionally plans* our steps to make certain these encounters are unavoidable.

God doesn't do this to provide us with a guilt trip; He does it to present us with an *opportunity*.

Opportunities often come packaged in ways we don't normally expect. We can get frustrated when it seems like God refuses to grant us an opportunity to serve Him. "Why won't God give me my big chance," we wonder. Then, we walk right by a poor, hungry soul, and . . . *miss our big opportunity*! You see, somewhere in life many of us got the idea that serving God is about preaching to stadiums overflowing with people or running around the jungles searching for heathens. However, the truth is, serving God is most often about simply caring enough to slow-down and help a fellow human being who is hurting. For most of us, our "big chance" happens *daily*, and we don't even notice!

This evening you will eat a full meal, and possibly even dessert. Meanwhile, your neighbor will have a big, fat bowl of *nothing*. Great news—this is *your opportunity*! How can you help? Buy and deliver a load of groceries and to them. Seeing their smile will be worth twice the price. Pinch your pennies by choosing generic brands for yourself, and then buy name-brand products for those in need. Invite them for dinner and listen to their story. You might be surprised to make a life-long friend!

Please don't misunderstand; I'm not trying to tell you how to run your life. But I do intend to bring to your attention the fact that, regardless of your financial situation, there are others who are in a deeper financial mess than you. In addition, I propose that there *is something* you can do to help them. Even if you can only help *one person* this month, that one person will go to bed thanking God for *you*. That's a good thing. Moreover, if the truth be told, it will do *you* more good than it will do *them*. Your kind act will fill their stomach with food, but it will fill your heart with joy. Couldn't you use a little more joy in your life? We all could.

However, this is not to say it will be convenient. Helping others never is. It will often cause you to go out of your way, or it will interrupt your patterned lifestyle. Jesus' story demonstrates this. From time to time, we are all guilty of wanting to continue on our journey without the inconvenience of stopping to help somebody else who was wounded on theirs. From a *cost-analysis* perspective, it seems we would be losing time and money by our efforts to stop and help. However, from a *risk-analysis* standpoint, we can't afford to *not* stop and help.

The Book of Proverbs declares, "Whoever shuts his ears to the cry of the poor will also cry himself and not be heard" (Proverbs 21:13, NKJV). Hard times *will fall* upon *everybody* in some way, shape, or form. This includes you and it includes me. If we choose to *not* help others going through their difficulties, then likewise, *we* will not receive help when we find ourselves in our own mess. This should encourage us to do *what* we can *when* we can. James goes even further, implying that earthly diseases can be the result of *hording* instead of *helping* (see James 5:3, and Psalm 41:1–3).

You see, there is good reason for the guilt we feel when we don't help someone we should. Guilt is an internal mechanism which prompts us to do what we already know is right, *and* informs us when we have ethically or morally failed. Our felt guilt is the *proof* of our choice to shirk the responsibility of being a real neighbor. However, as you can see, the stakes are much too high to ignore this facet of our Christian obligation. Jesus finished His story of the kind neighbor with the specific command to, "Go and do likewise" (Luke 10:37, NKJV). With so much at risk, we can't afford *not* to.

At this point, many of us are thinking: "How am I supposed to get anywhere in life if I am always making these pit-stops to help somebody?" I got to this point a few years ago. In my effort to obey this precept, I found myself stopping to help everybody in a pickle (in my earnestness, I even got "taken" by some con-jobs). Frustrated, I concluded that God either wanted me to be filthy-rich so I could fix everybody's monetary problems, or He wanted me to be dirt-poor so I would honestly have no resources to help anybody. I was in a conundrum. Then God gave me His answer through a Scripture: "But rather *give alms [charitable gifts of monetary help] of such things as you have*; then indeed *all things are clean to you*" (Luke 11:41, NKJV, emphasis added). You see, your job is not to "fix the world." Neither is mine. Our job is merely *to use what we have available to help the hurting people on our path.*

Some Christians will argue that helping the needy is the duty of the *church,* not the individual. Actually, it is the job of the church and the individual *both.* According to the New Testament epistles, the *only* recorded instances of first century church offerings being taken were for the purposes of *helping the poor and needy.* In addition, the early church leaders at Jerusalem, each personally trained to do ministry by the Lord Jesus Christ in the flesh, had a different way to take offerings than we find today. Each church member contributed to the "offering plate" *whatever they were pleased to give* (no "10 percent" mandates), then (gasp!) *each person took from the offering plate what they needed* (see Acts 4:34–37). Wow—thing have changed *a lot* in 2,000 years! Try taking a handful of cash from the offering plate this Sunday and you'll earn a "do not pass go" trip to jail! Also interesting is the frequency with which the "God loves a cheerful giver" and "he who sows sparingly will also reap sparingly" Scriptures are used to persuade people into giving to the local church (2 Corinthians 9:6–7, NKJV). Typically the offering-takers neglect to mention the fact that in the Bible these verses are not used in the context of giving to the institutional church, but in the context of giving *to the poor*. What this means is that, according to these passages, your level of "reaping" (the amount of reward you receive) is not based on what you give to the institutional church, but it is based on what you give *to the poor and needy*. Are you beginning to see a theme develop?

To this point, I challenge church leaders and members alike to analyze their church financial statements. Take note of the operating budget, and discover how much money actually goes to help the poor and needy. You will probably be surprised at the miniscule amount. "Clothing closets" and "food pantries" cannot be honestly counted, because they contain items donated by second-hand stores and local grocers. If the church institution did not pay for an item, then it cannot rightfully take credit for providing it from its budget. I'm talking about *real church money* used to pay a widow's electricity bill, or to cover the food expenses for a struggling family.

When the original Jerusalem Apostles sent-out the Apostle Paul to the gentiles, they gave him only one instruction: *"remember the poor"* (Galatians 2:10, NKJV, emphasis added). Look, I'm not making this stuff up—it's right there in the Bible! It seems that something so obviously important to the first century churches, as well as to Jesus Himself (see Luke 4:18), should find a place in the hearts of congregations today. Sadly, however, many institutional churches have *de*-volved from being *producers* to being *consumers*. They *take*, but do not *give back*.

Further, many churches have not instilled in the average con-gregant the knowledge that caring for others is part-and-parcel to a Christian's duty. This brings further injury to the needy person, as they can neither find assistance from the local institutional church, nor from their Christian neighbors who attend there. The Apostle James taught,

"If a brother or sister is naked and destitute of daily food, and one of you says to them, 'Depart in peace, be warmed and filled,' but you do not *give them* the things which are needed for the body, what *does* it profit?" (James 2:15–16, NKJV, emphasis added). This Christian duty was important enough for the first century church leaders to teach, and it should be important enough to teach today, also.

When needy folks cannot find help from the Christian church or their Christian neighbors, where else are they supposed to turn . . . *to the government?* It has become almost fashionable to complain of the growing size of the Federal Government's assistance programs. However, few people appreciate that the government is largely just assuming the duties which the local church has neglected. I thank the Lord for a government that cares more about the well-being of its people than most churches do. And *shame on us church-folk* for relinquishing to the government the noble calling of helping society's poor. Instead of investing in grander buildings and mini-kingdoms, maybe the church-at-large should invest in the grandest creation of all—*people.*

For several years my wife and I had tithed religiously to our local church. Our church hammered on the topic, and so for us it was a solid institution. I even tithed on the change I picked-up off the ground! But then there came a day of decision. As a full-time student, my complete household income was about $500 a month, of which we tithed $50. But when our neighbors entered a worse financial situation than us, we were left with a very difficult choice. Should we tithe to the church, as was our practice, or should we help our neighbors with that $50?

We asked the Lord in prayer what He wanted us to do about our predicament. To our dismay, we received no definitive answer from heaven. However, we did notice our local church comfortably nestled in a *multi*-million dollar facility complex, complete with new luxury automobiles in the staff parking lot. Then we looked at our Christian neighbors with three children and no food to eat. The contrast was disturbing, to say the least.

I admit that I did not want to tarnish my perfect tithing record. Moreover, if my wife and I would have had enough money to tithe to the organizational church, and still help the members of the Body of Christ, we would have done both. Nevertheless, we didn't; we had to choose one or the other. After much prayer and consideration, we realized that we could not joyfully give our tithe to a church organization, all the while knowing that our neighbor's children would not eat that week. So, we used our tithe money to buy as many groceries as $50 would buy, and delivered them to our hungry neighbors. They were *elated* to have those few meager bags of food. And to my amazement, the multi-million-dollar institutional church facility did not crumble that month! With this, I began to consider what was more important to God: financing a church organization and massive buildings, or providing food for God's people.

In all honesty we expected God to convict us of sin for not giving our $50 to our local church that month. When He did not, however, we were baffled. Only later did we learn the reason: it was because we unknowingly followed *the biblical model.* Let me show you what I mean.

Jesus was walking with His disciples on the Sabbath day, and His disciples were rubbing grain between their hands to eat. The Pharisees accused those disciples of breaking the Sabbath-day commandment, since rubbing grain between their hands constituted "work," which was illegal on the Sabbath. However, Jesus defended the disciples, saying:

> Have you never read what David did when he was in need and hungry, he and those with him: how he went into the house of God *in the days* of Abiathar the high priest, and ate the showbread, which is not lawful to eat except for the priests, and also gave some to those who were with him? . . . .The Sabbath was made for man, and not man for the Sabbath. Therefore the Son of Man is also Lord of the Sabbath (Mark 2:25–28, NKJV).

Jesus did not defend His disciples from the charge of Sabbath-breaking. Yet, neither did He criticize them for their actions, since they were acting out of hunger. Instead, Jesus linked this incident with an Old Testament passage in which the yet-to-be-king David was also hungry, and he also broke the law by eating the priest's bread. Because both of these parties acted to satisfy a legitimate need, Jesus insisted that both parties were to be held guiltless. You see, it all boils-down to *priorities*, and a person's well-being is a higher priority than an institutional regulation. Without realizing it, I had followed Jesus' example of *prioritizing people above institutions.*

My point is this: don't let someone else tell you where to invest your *Christian giving—you* take charge of it. It is not good enough to drop your tithe at church and expect God to be pleased while you ignore the poor and needy all around you. *You* are responsible before God to do rightly with that which is in your hand, and you cannot delegate this responsibility to another person . . . even if they do have a religious title.

Besides, church leaders are not immune to *doctrinal deficiencies*, and especially when it comes to money. Those who are paid by the organization have a vested interest in that organization. This interest has the potential to turn "kingdom men" into "company men." I've seen it happen. This was the problem of the two *religious leaders* (the priest and the Levite) who passed-by their injured brother on the road in Jesus' story. They esteemed the institutional organization as being more important than its individual members. It was only the *lay-person* who truly understood God's priorities, and it was *his* example (not that of the religious leaders) which Jesus commanded us to follow.

In addition, don't assume that all church leaders have the *right priorities*. Most do truly care for people, but there are still some proverbial "wolf in sheep's clothing" con-people in pulpits today. These preachers have seared their consciences to feel no regret when they swindle poor grandmothers out of their social security checks (see Matthew 23:14). How should congregations combat this threat? Perhaps the best idea might be to pay the pastor the median income of the church members. This would ensure that the pastor is never "out of touch" with the financial needs of the church members, in addition to leaving little incentive for wolf-like con-men to hang around. Even the mere suggestion of this would likely scare away many con-preachers looking to get rich off of poor congregants.

I believe it is a good standard practice for Christians to give 10 percent (or more, if so inclined) of their income for God's purposes. Moreover, how to allocate these funds is ultimately the *individual's* responsibility, and it should include elements of *both* supporting the local institutional church *and* helping those in need. It is right to give to the local assembly where you enjoy instruction, and you should be able to joyfully give to a ministry you truly believe in. However, to give to the institutional church at the expense of the poor and needy people on one's path is nothing short of a scandal. Jesus condemned the religious leaders of His day for this very practice: "But woe to you Pharisees! For you tithe mint and rue and all manner of herbs, and pass by justice and the love of God. *These you ought to have done, without leaving the others undone*" (Luke 11:42, NKJV, emphasis added). The context of this verse indicates that the "love of God" which Jesus here described was not merely a compassionate heart, but *the act of giving* by a compassionate heart.

In this passage the Lord Jesus Christ forever answered the question of: what is more important, to support God's religious establishment or to help the needy individual? His answer: don't neglect either—they are *both* important. Furthermore, it should be noted that by giving to Christians you *are* giving to the Church, because the true Church is not a building or an organization—*it is the people of God.* The first century church accepted this as truth, and the twenty-first century church would be wise to do the same.

Although our Lord's command to help the poor and needy should suffice, sometimes we need a little more motivation to spur us on to obedience. This is because we are humans, each with a sin-nature which seeks to inhibit our efforts to do what is right. So, in this case God obliges, with the added enticement of answered prayer. If you are rich in kindness, giving to those who have need, then God is more likely to grant your own prayer requests. According to the Apostle John:

> But whoever has this world's goods, and sees his brother in need, and shuts up his heart from him, how does the love of God abide in him? My little children, let us not love in word or in tongue, but in deed and in truth. And by this we know that we are of the truth, and shall assure our hearts before him. . . . And whatever we ask we receive from Him, *because we keep his commandments and do those things that are pleasing in His sight* (1 John 3:17–19, and 22, NKJV, emphasis added).

The point is this: if you want God to answer *your* prayer, then *you* become the answer to *someone else's.* This does not guarantee that your situation will turn-around on a dime, but it will demonstrate that you are a true child of God. This might even be the reason why your own personal trial has not yet been relieved. Maybe God is waiting for you to choose to be a blessing to someone else before He blesses you with your own open door.

To keep this practice of giving in balance, remember that God wants you to assist others with *some* of what you have; not *all* you have, or *more than* you have. If you stay within your abilities, you won't feel strained by the practice of helping others. Buy them groceries, give them some needed clothes, or secretly slip a $20-bill (or a $100-bill!) under their front door. Their heart will sing thanks to the Lord, and you will reap a harvest of joy *in spades.*

The message of this chapter is not a new concept, but it is an important one: *be a neighbor.* Be a real friend with someone who needs one. Lend a shoulder for someone to cry on, without telling them how to run their life. Help the broken and bruised person you happen upon today; they really are worse-off than you. You have probably wished, like I have, that somebody would throw you a bone in life, so throw someone else a bone. Stop waiting for *someone else* to treat you like a neighbor; instead, *you* become a neighbor for another hurting person. Eugene Peterson interprets Jesus' words like this: "Here is a simple rule of thumb for behavior: ask yourself what you want people to do for you; then grab the initiative and do it for *them!*" (Luke 6:31, *The Message*). Be for somebody else what you wish someone would be for you.

When should you start, and where? Start today, right where you are. Who should you help? You will recognize your opportunity when it presents itself. Remember, you don't need wealth to be a neighbor, but you do need a wealth of *kindness.* Compassion is *the crown of proof* that you are a child of the compassionate God (see Psalm 103:4). Don't go even *one more day* without this crown. Even if all you can afford to do is give a cup of cold water to someone, you will have a reward in heaven which outlasts the grandest buildings ever built (see Matthew 10:42). This will not only help the recipient, fill your heart with overflowing joy, *and* give you an eternal reward, but it will also make *you* a better person for it. And that's a good thing!

Discussion Questions

1. Have you found it easier to help others in today's difficult economy or back when America was doing better financially? Why?

2. Do you think of "opportunities" differently after reading this chapter? Why or why not?

3. Who do you know who is financially worse-off than you right now?

4. What practical things can you do to help that person or family?

5. The Bible speaks of benefits for those who help the poor. What are these benefits?

6. Whose job is it to help the poor and needy: the local church or the individual believer (or the Federal Government)? Explain.

7. Who is ultimately responsible for your giving? Has this insight caused you to reevaluate your giving strategy?

8. What is God's higher priority: the organizational church, or His people? Explain.

9. Has reading this chapter changed your attitude or opinion regarding giving to those in need? How so?

10. What practical changes will you make in your life as a result of reading this chapter?

11

Thank God for the Small Stuff

How to Get a New Heart

(DANIEL 6:10)

Nothing is so often irrevocably neglected as an opportunity of daily occurrence.

—MARIE VON EBNER-ESCHENBACH

INFORMATION CAN DRIVE A person to prayer. One example is when a person receives notification that their job has been terminated, or their retirement funds have been wiped-out. For the Christian, prayer is often one of our first responses to potentially-devastating news. This is because we are convinced that we have a Father in heaven who is concerned about our well-being. We know and trust that God cares for us, so we ask for His guidance and divine help in finding other work. This is a wonderful truth which the rest of the world does not have. Prayer is a guaranteed place of refuge from the storms of life. It is a place where we can separate ourselves from the pain of life, and immerse ourselves in God's loving presence. So while we search for another job, we pray.

As the months wear-on, we continue to do everything possible to find another job, albeit often without success. However, we want to cover *all* of our bases, so we continue to pray. We accept that our next job is in God's hands, so we dutifully offer our job-petition before Him hour after hour, and day after day.

Financial advisors often recommend having three-to-six months of reserve funds on-hand for emergencies like a job loss. Hopefully we have some monetary reserves to support us through our difficult transition periods. But the truth is many of us don't, which makes life even more difficult. To compound the problem, employment transitions take time, since good jobs have become scarce. With this in mind, even if you have a three-to-six month window (which most of us don't), there is no guarantee you will find another equal-pay job within that time. Often it takes longer. Moreover, as more time goes by, the root of discouragement grows deeper, making it even harder to uproot.

A person's rate of discouragement depends upon the individual. Typically, we feel the pinch as our back-up resources (whatever they may be) are squeezed. This pain affects each of us at a different rate, since we each have different amounts of reserve funds, and differing tolerance thresholds. But the truth is we *all* have our limit. As Christians, we *believe* that we trust God more than money. However, the fact is none of us *truly know* where our trust lies until we lose our worldly resources. None of us knows what metal we are made of until we are put into the fire for testing. Only then do we discover our limits. And when we reach our own personal limits, something inside us changes. It's like a switch that clicks from one position to the other. I call this the *attitude switch*.

The *attitude switch* regulates the signals which we are all constantly emitting to heaven. Although our personal attitude signals can never be *stopped*, the attitude switch can *adjust* them. You might guess that the two positions of the attitude switch are *thankfulness* and *unthankfulness* . . . but you'd be wrong. The two positions are *thankfulness* and *complaining*.

You see, as much as we might like to argue for it, there is really no middle-ground between these two positions. If we are not *actively thanking God* for the benefit of His involvement in our lives, then we are *actively grumbling against Him* for His apparent lack of involvement in our lives. We find this in the book of Exodus; in one moment the children of Israel praised God for His mighty acts, and the very next moment they complained about something which He had not yet done for them. The question we must each ask ourselves is: *which* of these two signals am I sending?

A few years ago I was sending only signals of thankfulness to God. I brought home nearly six-figures a year, and still had time to take a six-month vacation. I was *thankful*. It's *easy* to be thankful when life is going swell. But then I heard God's call to Bible school. I became excited; the Lord wanted to use me for something! I was more than just thankful—I was *ecstatic*! I learned and grew tremendously for two years into seminary. I was still thankful. My wife and I witnessed God faithfully and miraculously provide for all of our needs throughout those two years. We were blessed and we were thankful. With this past experience in mind, we felt assured that God's provision would continue through the last year of school. And for this we were also *thankful*.

For that last year, however, something changed. Our finances did not arrive as we expected, and times got tough. We remained diligent in prayer, and were still thankful. We jumped, we shouted, we prayed, and we fasted for our resources to arrive in the form of a job, or some other means. Nevertheless, our circumstances continued to degenerate. Being convinced God would come through for us, we waited expectantly for our miracle. Still, no miracle came. We looked to heaven for answers, but received none. We felt abandoned by God, and sunk into depression. Before we knew it, we stopped thanking God, and started *complaining*.

When complaining begins, it quickly multiplies. We *grumbled* that God had not provided for us. We *accused* God of blessing the wicked, while leaving His children without help. We *complained* that God no longer cares for us, all the while continuing to pray that He would meet our needs. However, our prayers were nothing more than disguised demands. We *insisted* that God act on our behalf. We *demanded* our right to provision. We firmly *claimed* our miracle. And while we were resolute in our requests, *we were not thankful*. It was a struggle to keep our family fed. Paying bills was impossible. Debt collectors called hourly. And most of our friends had abandoned us. We saw nothing to be thankful for. By then, even the shortest prayers, and the quickest devotionals were only a burden. We were fed-up. Maybe you are there right now.

During one of these dark days, I recalled the Old Testament story about my namesake, Daniel. Shortly after the lion's-den-conspiracy was hatched, the Bible gives us this insight into Daniel's life: "Now when Daniel knew that the writing was signed, he went home. And in his upper room, with his windows open toward Jerusalem, *he knelt down on his knees three times that day*, and prayed and *gave thanks* before his God, as was his custom since the early days" (Daniel 6:10, NKJV, emphasis added). The more I investigated this verse, the more intrigued I became.

Daniel had *just learned* that within a day or two his flesh would be torn from his body by hungry lions, yet he *still* found the nerve to *thank God*! Remember, up to this point in history, nobody had ever lived through a hungry-lions-sleep-over. Daniel had *no idea*, much less any guarantee, that God would perform a miracle to shut the lion's mouths and save him. Even so, he *still* kneeled down and prayed three times a day, just as he always had. For him life went from 60-mph to zero in a heartbeat, but Daniel refused to let this stop him from *thanking God.*

It occurred to me that there was a lesson I needed to learn from this verse. It seemed a little crazy, but I was out of all *rational* alternatives. I figured that if Daniel could thank God as he faced a den of hungry lions ready to chew him to pieces, then I could thank God as I faced the ravenous debt-collectors ready to eat me alive, too. So I tried it. Three times a day I got down on my knees and thanked God.

The truth is I did not look forward to these little chats. In fact, I felt nearly altogether disenfranchised with God at that point. It's not that I was giving-up on the Lord; it's that I thought He had already given-up on *me*. Moreover, since our relationship was already strained, I thought it would be best to lay-down some ground rules so *both of us* knew what to expect. I limited this three-prayer regimen to brief one-minute prayers: sixty-seconds in the morning, sixty-seconds at lunch time, and sixty-seconds at night. I figured that my list of thanks was so short it would be difficult to fill an entire minute, but I decided this should be my goal. Furthermore, I determined to follow Daniel's pattern as closely as possible, so I actually *knelt down* for these prayers. And since Daniel did not advertise his prayers, I concluded that mine must also be kept secret. Lastly, I resolved to bring *no request* to God whatsoever during these times. Instead, I would only *give thanks* to God . . . for *something.*

At first it was hard to remember my prayer times, as is the difficulty in forming any new habit. To keep my appointment, I would jot a note of reminder in my daily planner, or on scratch paper. The next difficulty was in finding a secret, yet suitable, place to kneel down for these short prayers. At our small apartment I could lock myself in the bathroom, but what about at work? Well, I just did the best I could. If nobody else was in the break-room, I would kneel in the far corner. And when somebody *did* walk-in on me (which happened several times), I would quickly jump to my feet and pretend like I was picking-up something from the floor. When the break-room was occupied during my 15-minute lunch-break, I would find a lonely restroom, kneel in a stall, and *hope* for 60-seconds of privacy while I prayed. It may not have been the most pleasant arrangement, but kneeling before God is never about maintaining one's dignity. To the contrary, it is about abasing ones' self before the Lord.

The spiritual aspects of this arrangement were interesting. At first I could only find three items to thank God for: life, salvation, and family. And each of these was repeated several times to fill the sixty-seconds. Then, after a few days I grew tired of restating the same three items, so I added a few others into the mix. But please don't think I was a spiritual giant after only three days—far from it! These additions were not the product of remarkable thoughts on my account. In fact they were almost childish. I thanked God for food to eat, water to drink, and air to breathe. I felt it was silly to thank God for such obvious and abundant resources. However, my heart was somehow stirred. So I continued.

Over the next few days I added love, peace, hope, and joy to my list of thanks. My heart responded positively to these, also. Over the following weeks I continued to practice my daily prayer regimen—as a *religious duty*. Then one day, a coworker said she noticed I was smiling more often. I hadn't thought about it until then. However, after she brought it to my attention, I even *caught myself* smiling more frequently. Next, I noticed that laughter came more easily than it had in recent months. It was about this time when I found myself becoming *anxious* for my next 60-second prayer time. I began to *crave* this private meeting with the God who loved me. It is important to notice that during this time, my situation had not changed in the slightest. The only difference was that *I had flipped my attitude switch*. You see, through this time God had been working on something much bigger than my circumstances; He had been working on my *heart*.

An attitude of thankfulness had completely replaced the grumbling spirit which I had carried for so long. No longer did I observe the things which God had *not yet* done for me. Instead, I saw the myriad of things which God had *already* done for me. Everywhere I looked I could find hints of God's overflowing love for me. Spring's blooming trees were a reminder that God is faithful to bring growth to areas of my life which had once appeared dead. The sunrise each day was my proof that God was still on-time and in-control of my personal world. The restful night-time was my own guarantee that God would grant me an appropriate period of rest after a long day of work. In everything I could find *something* to give thanks for, and thankfulness to God overflowed my heart all day long. This attitude even splashed-over into my relationships with others, resulting in a happier family and a more peaceful home.

The interesting thing is, it took near financial ruin for God to touch my heart deeply enough to make me truly thankful for His gifts of kindness. You see, I had based my security upon financial stability, instead of basing it upon God's promises. Yet without my trial this flaw in my heart would have never been revealed. Further, without addressing this root of the problem, my personal trust-issue would have never been remedied. Although I refused to admit it, throughout my prayer regimen I was secretly hoping that God would change my circumstances. But now I am thankful that He did not. *I needed* to come to terms with the fact that *my greatest need* was not a change of circumstances, but *a change of heart*. They were not *external* realities, but *internal* realities, which were causing my spiritual life to wither. However, God used this simple Daniel-prayer to breathe pure life into my relationship with Him once again. And I am *thankful*.

Paul declared the famous phrase, "I can do all things through Christ who strengthens me" (Philippians 4:13, NKJV) from a similar place in his life story. We like to quote this scripture as we face a difficult sporting activity, or maybe when we are up against a project deadline. Yet, in reality, this scripture has little to do with those things. Note the context: ". . . I have learned in whatever state I am, to be content. I know how to be abased, and I know how to abound. Everywhere and in all things I have learned both to be full and to be hungry, both to abound and to suffer need. I can do all things through Christ who strengthens me" (Philippians 4:11b-13, NKJV). Paul is stating that he has a source of strength which allows him to abound during good times and persevere through bad times; and that source is Jesus Christ. No sporting events are mentioned. No business projects inferred. This Scripture passage is simply about *getting through tough life circumstances*. And Paul successfully navigated through his difficult times by leaning on the strength which Christ gave him.

Have you been complaining about what God has *not yet* done for you, instead of thanking God for what He has *already* done for you? You are not alone. I certainly don't want you to feel condemned, but I do want to *challenge* you, just as God challenged me. You see, your heavenly Father has something better planned for your life than the unthankful grumblings which often accompany life's difficulties. His plan is for you to be thankful and filled with His joy as you overcome life's troubles.

The Old Testament prophet Habakkuk said it like this: "Though the fig tree may not blossom, nor fruit be on the vines; though the labor of the olive may fail, and the field yield no food; though the flock may be cut off from the fold, and there be no herd in the stalls—yet I will rejoice in the LORD, I will joy in the God of my salvation. The LORD God is my strength; He will make my feet like deer's *feet*, and He will make me walk on my high hills" (Habakkuk 3:17–19, NKJV). Habakkuk had determined that even if he had no provisions for life, He would still rejoice in the Lord and thereby overcome any situation. He had the right attitude.

By now we know that God can speak a simple word and thereby fix all of our financial strains forever. However, fixing our *financial* problem would do nothing toward fixing our *heart-attitude* problem. And clearly the latter is more important to God. Moreover, it should be clear that God is using your struggles to challenge you to become a better *you*—someone who trusts God far beyond what you can see with the human eye, just as Daniel did. The Lord wants you to overcome all attitude-deficiencies. Otherwise these deficiencies will continue to be like a spiritual chain tied around your feet, hindering you from forward progress and blocking your potential. There is more for you in life than what you have already seen, but you need to get rid of your unthankfulness-chain to get there.

If life stinks for you right now, I urge you to *take the "three-minute Daniel challenge."* Find a quiet spot and kneel before your God three times a day, committing to pray for 1-minute each time. You will probably have to be creative when looking for a place and time to kneel before the Lord, just as I did. Please be advised, in this exercise it is vital that you *do not ask for anything.* This is not about coaxing God to do your will or to change your circumstances. It is about something *much bigger*: it is about *changing your heart.*

Make it a point to express thankfulness to your Lord for anything and everything which comes to mind. It is a conversation between only you and God, so don't be shy. There is no "right" prayer or "wrong" prayer . . . there is only *your* prayer. Let it come from your heart and make it your own. You can't go wrong by investing three minutes a day. Please realize, I cannot promise that your circumstances will be changed in three minutes a day. In fact, they probably won't. However, I *can* guarantee that before you know it, *you* will be changed. You have nothing to lose, but a new heart to gain! If you will commit to take this one small step, then you will have made a giant leap toward becoming *better for life.*

Discussion Questions

1. Is it true that *everybody has their limit*? Why or why not.

2. What is the *one way* that a Christian determines what they are basing their trust on? Explain.

3. Based upon your current (or past) situations, how would you describe your own personal "rate of discouragement"? Why?

4. Explain the "attitude switch." What are the two positions of this *switch*?

5. Regarding your own *attitude switch*, what signals have you been sending?

6. Were you able to connect with the Daniel story in this chapter? How so?

7. After reading this chapter, what would you identify as your *greatest* need?

8. Do you see the benefit of the three-minute *Daniel-prayer-challenge*? Explain.

9. Will you personally commit to this prayer-challenge? What do you expect to get out of it?

12

Grow Up

How to Be an "Always-the-More" Christian

(MATTHEW 26:36–46)

"My will, not thine, be done," turned Paradise into a desert.
"Thy will, not mine, be done," turned the desert into a paradise,
and made Gethsemane the gate of heaven.

—EDMOND DE PRESSENSE

LONELINESS INTENSIFIES SORRY AND pain. Probably one of the toughest aspects of trials is the fact that we each have to face ours completely alone. Maybe you have experienced this extent of loneliness. If so, it probably seems like your family has denied you and your friends have abandoned you. Beyond being lonely, the darkness comes. It feels like evil has surrounded you, leaving you no escape. Your life is overcast with *darkness*, and your heart is inundated with *loneliness*. And there is no way out. Your only recourse is to pray for it to stop. Have you been there?

You should know that you're not alone in your experience. The Lord Jesus Christ went through the *exact same thing* when all of His friends abandoned Him at the Garden of Gethsemane. At the darkest hour of the darkest night of His life . . . He was *alone*. Upon His shoulders He bore the tremendous weight of the sin of the world. Meanwhile, He was surrounded by all the evil hell could muster together. And out of all of His life and trials, *nothing* compared to what He experienced this last night of His life.

Then Jesus came with them to a place called Gethsemane, and said to the disciples, "Sit here while I go and pray over there." And He took with Him Peter and the two sons of Zebedee, and He began to be sorrowful and deeply distressed. Then He said to them, "My soul is exceedingly sorrowful, even to death. Stay here and watch with Me." He went a little farther and fell on His face, and prayed, saying, "O My Father, if it is possible, let this cup pass from Me; nevertheless, not as I will, but as You *will*." Then He came to the disciples and found them sleeping, and said to Peter, "What! Could you not watch with Me one hour? Watch and pray, lest you enter into temptation. The spirit indeed is willing, but the flesh *is* weak." Again, a second time, He went away and prayed, saying, "O My Father, if this cup cannot pass away from Me unless I drink it, Your will be done." And He came and found them asleep again, for their eyes were heavy. So He left them, went away again, and prayed the third time, saying the same words (Matthew 26:36–44, NKJV).

Have you ever wondered why Jesus did it? He purchased the salvation for mankind on a cross at a place called Golgotha. So, why did He go through this agony of suffering at *Gethsemane*? More specifically, why did He go through all of it *for you* and *for me*? As silly as it may sound, I have pondered over this very question literally hundreds of times, but only recently have I realized the answer. My reason for struggling with this question is because I view this as the crux of all practical Christian teaching. In my opinion, it is the single greatest divisive issue in all Protestantism.

Each Christian carries in them an answer to this question, whether they realize it or not. Moreover, a person's answer to this question will determine their inward expectations of Christianity, their outward practice thereof, and it will even determine their choice of churches. It determines what Christian authors the individual will read, and what teachers they will listen to. It even provides the lens through which the believer views material goods and physical comforts alike. In short, the answer to "why did Jesus suffer for me?" permeates *every aspect of a believer's life and faith*.

The Bible only truly supports two answers to this question. Answer #1: Jesus suffered for me *so I don't have to suffer now*, but that I might reign in life. Answer #2: Jesus suffered for me *so I can follow His example of suffering now*, and reign in the *after*life. There is clearly a difference between these two answers, making it impossible to simultaneously embrace both. Like the Great Divide, all Christendom falls on the side of one answer, or on the side of the other.

Yet as different as these answers are, both have biblical support, and both are doctrinally sound. Further, every Christian falls into one camp or the other, including you and me. However, during our lifetimes every one of us must make the doctrinal leap from one camp to the other, and your difficulties are God's way of challenging you to make this jump. Let me show you what I mean.

For years I was an Answer #1-guy. I embraced the answer which my church taught: Jesus suffered for me so I don't have to suffer. This was reflected in my attitude and lifestyle. I expected life's best. After all, as a Christian I am a "King's Kid." I expected favor in the job market, imagining that employers were salivating to add me to their payrolls. I expected to drive new luxury automobiles sporting God-slogan license plates as a testimonial to all those I flew past on the road. I thought I deserved to own a grandiose home—to testify of God's goodness to my neighbors. Further, wearing thousand-dollar suits would provide me the opportunity to tell the grocery store clerk about the benefits of following Christ. Beyond my own lavish expenses, I expected to have an overflow of income so I could finance *God's* enterprises.

The Bible says that God owns the cattle on a thousand hills (Psalm 50:10), so I figured He surely wouldn't mind sparing a few calves for one of His own very special children. Certainly He wants the best for us, I reasoned, and He already paid a high price to give it to us! If you are an Answer #1-person, then you recognize the same elements in your own belief system, albeit maybe to a different extent. My #1 Answer affected my *belief system*, and my belief system affected my *attitudes*, and my attitudes affected my *actions*. I expected the world to be at my beck and call, serving my needs and desires. And since I made plenty of cash, this answer worked for me.

Then I quit my job to attend seminary, and I encountered financial hardship. When this happened, my #1 Answer also affected my reactions. For example, since I was a King's Kid, I expected to make a substantial amount on a quick sale of my home. Yet since I could no longer afford my home, I was now facing foreclosure. I could not even find someone to buy it for what I owed! In my mind this was absolutely unsatisfactory for a King's Kid! So I fought back.

I was convinced Satan's kingdom was to blame, so I rebuked the devil and his minions who were trying to ruin my financial life and take my financial blessings. After all, God *gave me* my stuff, and I was not about to let Satan (and the bank) take it! When I was done rebuking, I prayed and fasted for *God's favor* to sell our home. I felt certain God would come through for me, and all my woes would be relieved by a fast sale. Just as Jesus did in the Garden of Gethsemane on the eve before His death, from the depths of my heart I pleaded that God would "take this cup from away me" (Mark 14:36, NKJV). I was praying that He would "fix" my problems.

It is important to recognize that Jesus did not merely use words to teach; He taught with His actions, also. This makes it all the more significant that Jesus intentionally brought three disciples (Peter, James and, John) with Him at His most trying hour. He *wanted* these three disciples to see Him agonize with the decision to trust His heavenly Father, as He stepped into the darkest portion of His life. It was extremely difficult for Jesus to make this decision, which is what His Garden of Gethsemane experience was all about. He *struggled* to trust His heavenly Father when He knew it would cost His own *life*. Yet, as the Master Teacher, He *needed* those three disciples to *watch Him* agonize over God's will for His life, so when they later found themselves in dark moments they would recall Jesus' example and follow suit. Likewise, as you and I (later disciples of Christ) read the writings of Peter, James, and John, we can see how they handled *their* trials, and we can follow their example, also.

As I sat in the darkness of my most trying hour, with the weight of financial ruin bearing down upon my shoulders, I echoed Jesus' prayer: "take this cup from me." I prayed this for nearly a full year. But the cup did not pass. When I realized that God would not take the cup from me, I fell into despair. Since I was a #1-Answer guy, believing that *Jesus suffered so I would not have to*, my only option was to question God's love for me. My #1 Answer determined what level of provision I expected to receive from God. However, since I was not *receiving* that level of provision, maybe God didn't really love me, I reasoned. Maybe I was not a *real* "Kings Kid" after all. I wondered if maybe I had just been fooling myself all along. Have you ever believed that your efforts to pursue God were not reciprocated by Him? My #1 Answer forced me there. If you are an Answer #1-person going through turmoil, then your answer has forced you there, also.

As my trials continued, I began to reevaluate my answer to the question: "why did Jesus suffer for me?" This was necessary, since my *expectation* did not match my *experience*. Even more than I needed resolution to my financial struggles, I needed resolution to my *doctrinal* struggle. In other words, *I needed to know that God loved me even through* my circumstances. For months I agonized over the inconsistency which my #1 Answer, in combination with my terrible circumstances, produced. Without resolution, I was in danger of throwing-in the towel, alleging that Christianity only works for the rich.

However, the more I wrestled with it, the more I began to see that Jesus Christ is to be our *example*. The Apostle Peter wrote, "For to this were you called, because Christ also suffered for us, *leaving us an example, that you should follow His steps*" (1 Peter 2:21, NKJV, emphasis added). Moreover, as His followers, we are supposed to do things *His* way, whether this leads to abundance or whether it leads to death (John 21:18–23). I realized that Answer #2, "Jesus suffered for me so I can now follow His example of suffering," fit both the Scriptures and my experience. So I made the jump to embrace Answer #2.

This was a difficult transition to make. Part of this transition included leaving the church which I had attended for years, as it was a firm proponent of Answer #1. I found I could not listen to the incessant preaching of the *non*-suffering Christian life while I was *suffering*. So I found another church-home which embraced Answer #2. Another change was that I found it necessary to revisit many Bible passages which I thought I understood. Now I would allow this new view to readjust my understandings of those passages accordingly. As if this was not enough, my new answer also impressed me to *change my lifestyle*.

I realized I could no longer "name and claim" the solutions to my problems. No longer could I expect God to fix my problems by pushing gobs of money out of heaven's windows and into my life. I had to stop accusing the devil of taking my stuff, and accept the fact that I had chosen to live above the means which God provided. Moreover, I had to accept that although Jesus was *already* Ruler of *my life*, He was *not yet* the ruler of *this world*—Satan still holds that title (see John 12:31). So, instead of expecting the world to be at my beck and call, I realized I was called to humble myself and serve others, and thereby follow the example of the Lord Jesus Christ (Philippians 2:5–8).

With this knowledge, I disenrolled myself from the *King's-Kid-Entitlement-Program*, and began learning to be content with the little which God put into my hand. In doing this, I let the Lord be *Lord* of my life, releasing all control of my life and future to God. In short, I had finally embraced the *second half* of Jesus' Gethsemane prayer: "nevertheless, not as I will, but as You *will*" (Matthew 26:39, NKJV). And as I prayed this *complete* prayer, the peace and love of God flooded my heart.

As I continued to pray this way, I found that my expectations changed. Instead of choosing a top job and praying for God's favor to land it, I began to ask the Lord to give me whatever position *He* wanted me to occupy. I concluded that if God wanted me in a particular place, He might intentionally block other employment avenues. So, instead of delivering my plans to God and expecting Him to carry-out my orders, I realized that my greatest need was for *God* to plan my life and to give me *His* orders. Through this I accepted that *God's plan was better* than my own.

Although I knew God's will would be painful in the short-term (just like it was with Jesus), I also knew it would be worth it in the long-term (see Philippians 2:9–11). I began to see that Jesus' blood-soaked Gethsemane prayer was not something which He did to make my life *easier*. Instead, it was something He did *to teach me* how to handle my own Gethsemane-experience, and thereby *grow-up* in the faith. This was indeed humbling. However, it was a healthy and life-giving step to release control of my life to the Lord of heaven and earth, who loved me and gave Himself for me.

By the grace of God it was done—I had leaped the chasm! Now I could finally see that the oft-important outward elements of life (like money, clothes, houses, etc.) are truly *un*important. Meanwhile, attributes which many people consider unimportant or even disdainful (like meekness, gentleness, kindness, faithfulness, etc.) are actually of *tremendous value*. The sleek cars and grand houses which once impressed me no longer did. And the things I used to scoff at now held my attention in rapt awe.

My personal benefit from this shift was *tremendous*. Since I now had a practicable theology which incorporated arbitrary suffering, I could accept the fact that *God still loved me*. Through my studies of biblical characters' difficulties, I understood that my trials *matched* biblical expectations. With this new information, I could finally put an end to the accusations from myself and others, alleging I was harboring hidden sins which were withholding my monetary blessings. This realization was refreshing, hope-building, and even *empowering*! Now I could truly see myself as someone who actually *followed* Jesus Christ.

I have learned it is easy to entice people to Christianity if they are promised a Rolex with matching car and mansion (i.e., Answer #1). Few come to Christ asking what *they* can do for *Him*. Most come only seeking what *He* can do for *them*. Yet sooner or later the Christian will face his or her personal Gethsemane. When this happens, the individual must reevaluate their reasons for following Christ, and ultimately make a decision to proceed with His program by embracing Answer #2. Gethsemane is a *stage* in the growth of a believer. It is a Bar/Bat-Mitzvah of sorts; a "coming of age" experience. It is the point in the Christian life when the individual believer *ceases* being an adolescent in the faith, and becomes a *full-grown spiritual adult*.

My wife and I were blessed with a baby girl one year ago. Ariel is my little princess, and my delight. Even after my most difficult days, I become instantly filled with happiness when I see her totter around the room, yelping for joy because her daddy is home. To her I am like a *rock-star*! The truth is my wife and I would do *anything* for our precious daughter. We provide for her physical needs of clothing, shelter, and food. She cries to notify us when she thinks she has a problem, and we come and address the need appropriately. If she is dirty, we clean her. If she is hurt, we bandage and comfort her. And this will continue for many pleasant years, I'm sure. Later, Ariel's car might break-down. She will call me, and I will fix that situation, just like I fix all other situations.

However, I know this phase of our relationship will not last forever. There will come a day when things *must* change. Although she will always be my princess, Ariel will grow-up and learn to be self-sufficient. She will choose her own college, and her own career, working hard to succeed in both. She may move to a different location, and trade her "rock-star" dad nostalgia for the joy of a good husband. And when her car breaks-down, instead of calling *me* to get it fixed, *she* will call the mechanic. In short, Ariel will make the noteworthy transition from being a young girl into being a mature woman. One day, my little princess will *grow-up*.

At some point in time each of us *must* undergo a similar transition in our spiritual lives. As new Christians, God takes care of us, just as any decent earthly father takes care of his little children. He carries us and holds us near. He protects us from harm, and shelters us from our fears. When we *do* fall down, or when bad things happen to us, God is right there to heal our heart and fix our problem. In essence, God answers every one of our "Let this cup pass from me" prayers when we are young Christians.

However, there comes a time in our spiritual growth when God, as a good and loving Father, expects us to transition from spiritual childhood into spiritual adulthood. He does not protect us to the same extent as when we were new to the faith, because He wants us to gain valuable life experience. No longer does He shield us so extensively from the world, because He wants us to learn to make good decisions. And He doesn't jump at each of our "Let this cup pass from me" cries, because God wants us to share in the work which Jesus Christ began.

To make this transition from spiritual adolescence to spiritual adulthood, God places us in our own agonizing Gethsemane-situation, where we have nowhere else to turn. Just like Jesus' Gethsemane experience, our friends abandon us and our enemies hunt us. No longer are our spiritual "mentors" available to hold our hands or answer our questions. And as the darkness presses in on every side, and the fear of evil threatens to engulf us, we pray the "help me" prayer which we have always prayed. But it does not work. In Gethsemane, God does not answer pleas for help. In Gethsemane, God's silence compels the individual to make the transition from spiritual adolescence into full spiritual adulthood. *So He waits.* He waits as long as it takes for us to learn the second half of our Teacher's prayer: ". . . nevertheless, not *my* will be done, but *Your* will be done." Only through this agonizing experience do we make the difficult transition into the spiritual adulthood.

As a general rule, each of us prays for our desired solutions to life's problems. And there is nothing wrong with this. Jesus Christ Himself modeled this as He prayed for "this cup to pass" from Him. However, Jesus did not end His prayer there, and neither should we. As the Son of God, Jesus did not have to *grow into* spiritual maturity at Gethsemane; He prayed the *full* prayer *every* time. However, as His followers we *do* have to grow into maturity. Yet, we make this transition when we embrace the "nevertheless" portion of Jesus' prayer for ourselves. By doing so, we acknowledge that we are not the all-knowing and all-powerful God of the universe, and we vocalize our acceptance of His plan, regardless of what it may be.

This acceptance does not come easily. In fact, we can only mature in this respect when we find ourselves in our own Gethsemane. If you have not yet been there, then be warned . . . it is coming. Every one of us *must* undergo our own Garden of Gethsemane experience, so we can face our *nevertheless* moment alone. There will be nobody else to seek help from but God Himself. Nobody else can step-in and relieve your fears or calm your heart. Further, no one but you can accept God's plan for your life. We each must learn to say (even for the first time), ". . . *nevertheless*, not my will be done, but Your will be done." Nobody can say it for you.

It's ok to agonize over this—Jesus did. It's alright to weep—so did Jesus. It's even ok to initially shy away from the cup of suffering in your hand. Even the Lord Jesus had to pray this prayer *three times* for it to finally be settled in His heart (Matthew 26:44). The point is this: although it will be difficult, *you can get through it*. You can succeed at anything which God puts in your path. You can even get through what you are facing now, *if* you will trust the Lord by adding your "nevertheless" disclaimer. You will have reached a major spiritual milestone when you finally kneel before your God and tell Him from the bottom of your heart, "Even if I never get what I want in life, I will still love You and worship You forever."

To most of us, a *nevertheless* prayer sounds somewhat negative; however, it is actually a *tremendous positive* in our spiritual lives. An alternate meaning of this word is: "always-the-more." It is a positive acknowledgement that God does indeed know more than we do, and that *we want "the more"* which He has available for us. By praying this, we wisely make the decision to *refuse "the less"* (i.e., that which we *assumed* was the best thing for us), choosing rather to ask God for "*the more*" (which is only known by God Himself). "Nevertheless" really means you are tired of settling for the dregs of the spiritual life, and from this moment on, you want God's "always-the-more" *best* plan to begin.

You see, *God has better plans for your life than you do!* You can trust Him with your future. He has been planning every detail of your "perfect life" for thousands of years, and has made every provision to ensure you receive this blessing. Therefore, while you are in your own Gethsemane, you have a choice to make: you can choose to ignore the second half of Jesus' prayer, and thereby settle for your "less" plan. Or you can pray this second portion of Jesus' prayer, and thereby step into the *always-the-more* future which God has planned for you. It's your choice.

My exhortation for you, while you are in your Gethsemane experience, is that you become an *always-the-more* Christian. Put your faith and hope in God's ability to lead you even through your midnight hour. When you face the toughest challenge of your life, and nobody else will stay awake with you, *trust God to get you through the darkness.* You may not realize it, but *He has a plan.* You can trust God. And don't think that I am only preaching this to you, because I am not. I am preaching this to *myself,* also.

Since I graduated from seminary over a year ago, my attempts to find a ministry position have been unsuccessful. Churches just don't want to take a chance on a new preacher like me. Even further, since church-giving has significantly decreased in this economy, few churches are hiring staff members—most are *firing* them. Although I have not wanted to revert to my previous engineering career, at this point, I have no other option. Therefore, I have again been praying for *never-the-less* in my prayers. Only God knows what His best plans for me are, and if He wants me to again practice engineering, I will obey.

With this in mind, I have interviewed for two different engineering jobs. However, my apartment rental agreement is about to expire, and my minimum-wage part-time job is about to end (again). Taking all of this into account, unless a miracle happens, I will move my family into a tent until a job offer comes along. I know this is not ideal, but it is the best we can manage for now. But we remain convinced that God loves us, and that Jesus will never forsake us. We will be alright. (And I'll bet Job *wished* he had a wife as supportive as mine!)

I don't write this for your pity; I write this for your encouragement. If my family and I can be content staring at a future in a three-person dome tent, then *you* can find a way to be content in *your* situation. God has not deserted you, and Jesus promised to never leave you. He loves you and will never stop loving you. And He wants to make you better. If you will submit to His plan, then He will make you an overcoming and victorious Christian. Instead of yielding to your situational fears, trust God to supply your *always-the-more* future, even if you don't understand it. *Don't settle for "the less" any longer.* Times may be tough, and they may get even tougher. But if you will commit to asking God for *never-the-less,* then you will experience God's *always-the-more* future for you. You can take that to the bank.

Discussion Questions

1. Do you find any similarities between your situation and Jesus' Garden of Gethsemane situation? Explain.

2. Before reading this chapter, what would have been your answer to the question, "Why did Jesus suffer for me?" How did this affect your attitudes and actions?

3. Has your answer to this question changed, based upon reading this chapter? Explain.

4. What transition happens when we choose to start praying the "nevertheless" portion of Jesus' prayer? What kind of changes can you expect this to make in your attitudes and actions?

5. How and why does God prompt a Christian to pray Jesus' "nevertheless" prayer?

6. Can you get through the Christian life without going through your own Gethsemane experience? Why or why not?

7. Have you found yourself praying your own "let this cup pass from me" prayer? Explain.

8. Discuss the second half of Jesus' Gethsemane prayer, and its importance in the Christian life.

9. What is another meaning of "nevertheless"? Explain what this means to you.

10. Will you commit to praying to become an "always-the-more" Christian? Why or why not?

13

Don't Just Sit There . . . Expand!

How to Change the World

(Acts 8:1–8)

A certain amount of opposition is of great help to a man.
Kites rise against, not with the wind.

—John Neal

COMFORT IS THE ENEMY of progress. There is an old saying that an individual won't change until the cost of remaining the same exceeds the cost of change. Even Sir Isaac Newton's First Law of Motion could easily be adapted to support this: *A man at rest on the couch will remain on the couch until his wife exerts a threat sufficient to budge him.* In other words, all of us tend towards comfort and routine.

For many of us comfort is our main goal in life, and we work hard to obtain it. However, when we finally do achieve our desired comfort-level, we typically stop striving. Our ambition is to sip tea, while nestled in a comfortable chair on our front porch retreat, and watch the sun set over a breathtaking view. When we reach this comfortable plateau, we stop climbing upwards towards the mountain peaks. We have *settled*. It's easy to settle.

Nearly 2000 years ago, the early church in Jerusalem had settled. Many consider this church to be the gold-standard of all churches. Even today, there is a movement to return to the model of this earlier church. Nonetheless, *it had settled*. The first six chapters of the book of the Acts of the Apostles describe this picture-perfect church. It was strong, sound, and vibrant. The Christians there boldly preached the message of Christ in the face of persecution, and won thousands of converts at a time (Acts 2:41). The sick and lame were healed by the mere shadow of some of the church leaders (Acts 3:6–10, and 5:15).

From the perspective of today's pastor, this was *the dream church.* With barely a schism, fellowship abounded throughout the church with no class distinctions. The ministry was grounded on prayer, and all the members were resolute in following their leaders' vision and instruction. Moreover, it was not uncommon for church members to sell their lands and joyfully give the entire proceeds to the church! (see Acts 4:34). This first church was strong and vibrant from every indication. And by any measure it appeared to be the "church victorious."

However, although every indicator showed this to be the church par excellence, something was missing. Without this one element, all of the good attributes and noble acts of this church would amount to nothing but a story in a book. It is no exaggeration to say that the existence of the entire Christian church as we know it hung in the balance. And the frightening thing is, *nobody there even realized it.* Nobody but God, that is. So God Himself took the initiative to give this near-perfect church the one blessing which they were in dire need of: *persecution.*

In our minds, persecution is the last thing we would think this fledgling church needed. After all, it was struggling for survival in a very difficult time and place in history. It would almost seem to be irresponsible for God to allow His new Church to be overwhelmed with harassment. Still, it was almost as if God stepped aside to allow the forces of darkness to devastate His brand-new Church. As a result, it looked as though the greatest church of all time had failed; the overcoming church had been overcome.

The book of the Acts of the Apostles records this persecution, which began at the stoning-death of Stephen, one of the church leaders. "And at that time a great persecution arose against the church which was at Jerusalem; and they were all scattered throughout the regions of Judea and Samaria, except the apostles. And devout men carried Stephen *to his burial,* and made great lamentation over him. As for Saul, he made havoc of the church, entering every house, and dragging off men and women, committing *them* to prison" (Acts 8:1–3, NKJV).

This persecution devastated the entire Christian community on its home turf. Christians lost their jobs, and were forcibly separated from their families, among other things. The same believers who were respected and feared by their community had now become the filth of society. They were branded as traitors and hunted from house to house. They were thrown in jail—and some were even executed. These appeared to be the darkest days of the church's short life. It looked as if the church would not survive. *Why would God allow persecution at this time?*

To be sure, it's not that God *wanted* persecution for His new Church. It was the means to the end, not the end itself. So, God *allowed* persecution in order to get what He *really* wanted. He used persecution to produce in His Church the *one crucial element* which it needed to survive the ages. He leveraged persecution to gain *expansion.*

Expansion is the highest goal and the greatest accomplishment of the Church. It is the very reason why the Son of God invaded planet earth, to set the prisoners free. Expansion is never easy, but it is always necessary for God's Church to survive. Without it, the Kingdom of God would quickly fade into a pathetic obscurity. Unless the Gospel of Jesus Christ is actively imparted to others, the Church is always only one generation away from complete extinction. If persecution had not forced the Jerusalem church to expand outside its walls, Christianity would have been nothing more than a one-generation hiccup in the history of Judaism.

Those early Christians probably did not understand the reason for their persecution, or the Church's need for expansion. They did not realize that Jerusalem would be sacked and the only Christianity which would survive the next twenty centuries is that which made it over Jerusalem's wall. However, since God's main purpose was to have His Church expand, He allowed persecution to fall upon that early church with full force. As a result, the early Christians were forcibly and fearfully dispersed throughout the known world. And thank God they were!

Not only did the Christian movement need expansion to survive, but it also needed expansion because the Gospel of Jesus Christ was *just too good* to keep within the walls of Jerusalem! Good news is neither *good* nor *news* for those who never hear it. If the Gospel had never made it out of Jerusalem, 99.9% of humans across the ages would never have known that Jesus Christ made the way for them to commune with God. The message *had* to make it over the Jerusalem wall! In fact, from the Church's inception, God planned this movement to spread from Jerusalem to the ends of the earth (Acts 1:8). God did not want a *Jerusalem* Church movement . . . He wanted a *worldwide* Church movement.

The American church today is in a similar predicament. Life within the American church is hardly suffering. As demonstrated by its plethora of denominations and ministries, the church is quite vibrant. The American church is considered the benchmark of spiritual success, as Christian leaders from all over the world look to it for wisdom and instruction. Bible colleges and seminaries abound in the U.S., from where the written Word of God is plentifully distributed. In the history of the world, there has never before amassed such a vast knowledge of the contents of the Bible as is found in the American church today.

We have biblical archaeology, apologetics, biblical languages, teaching ministries, evangelistic crusades, Christian radio, Christian television, Christian universities, and churches of every stripe and color dotting the American landscape from coast to coast. Arguably, never before has the Church been so intellectually educated, politically powerful, and man-power abundant. In a sentence, America has laborers coming out of its *ears*, while much of the rest of the world waits for a single messenger of hope to arrive. Furthermore, God's agenda for today's Church is no different than the mission of the early Jerusalem church: God still wants expansion.

A tree grows in several directions nearly simultaneously. Its roots grow deeper into the ground for stability and support of its above-ground appendages. Meanwhile its trunk and limbs grow taller and wider to extend over more ground area. Similarly, the Church of Jesus Christ grows in depth and by expansion, as cultivated by God Himself. During *depth-growth* seasons, the church grows in *depth*, to add stability and support to the trunk and branches. This is what the Jerusalem church was experiencing prior to the dispersion in Acts chapter 8, and it is what the American church has been experiencing for several decades. Additionally, there are other seasons when God expect His church to grow by *expansion*. During these *expansion-growth* seasons, God expects the branches to extend further and cover more ground area.

Both of these seasons facilitate growth, yet they facilitate different *types* of growth. In the first seven chapters of Act, the Jerusalem church was growing in depth at an astonishing rate. But it was hardly expanding outside of Jerusalem. It was disproportional; like a tiny tree with massive roots. Similarly, although depth-growth is clearly evident in the twentieth century American church, expansion-growth has only been modestly found in it. Quite possibly, *now* is the time for expansion. My point is this: maybe God has allowed today's financial crisis to disrupt American life for the purpose of thrusting the American church out of its comfort zone, and into the fray of the spiritual battle for lives. Battles are not won from the sidelines. And the world won't hear about Jesus Christ if the church continues to sit comfortably nestled watching the scenery. As a church, we have *settled*.

Unrest (coming in the form of persecution or financial distress) is God's gift to a stalled and settled church. Moreover, just like the church at Jerusalem, God is using America's crisis to upset our creature comforts, and incite us to bring His message of hope to the ends of the earth. The Church mission of Acts 1:8 has still not been fully accomplished! And as long as there remains work to be done, God will be faithful to send persecution (as with Jerusalem), or economic disruption (as with America), to keep His people focused on the mission. The Church's mission has never been to take-over a mere city; the Jerusalem story proves this. The mission has always been to *reach the world*, and it will take a collective effort of hard work to get it done.

For those inside the Jerusalem church, persecution probably felt more like collapse. It is likely that those who were scattered around the world considered the early Jerusalem church to be their glory days. They might have thought their persecution disrupted the church's success. Yet in fact, the very opposite was true. The dispersion *was* the church's success. From this point on, we find a church which did not settle for being limited to stay within a city wall. Believers were no longer content to keep "the Church" inside the church. Instead, they did whatever it took to carry the Gospel message to Judea and Samaria, and then full-swing towards the ends of the earth. One example of this mind-shift is seen in Philip.

> Therefore those who were scattered went everywhere preaching the word. Then Philip went down to the city of Samaria and preached Christ to them. And the multitudes with one accord heeded the things spoken by Philip, hearing and seeing the miracles which he did. For unclean spirits, crying with loud voice, came out of many who were possessed; and many who were paralyzed and lame were healed. And there was great joy in that city (Acts 8:4–8, NKJV).

Philip is just one example of the many people who did great things to further the kingdom of God during that early persecution. He is a striking example of somebody who was a *successful participant* in the Christian mission, because he used difficult circumstances as leverage to advance the kingdom of God. And the great news is *you* can do the same.

I realize today's circumstances are different from those of Philip's day. In America, we have no gripping fear of being jailed or killed for our faith in Christ. However, we do have other realities which inject fear into our minds. We are fearful of losing our jobs, worried about our weakened economy, and alarmed by our uncertain future. For many of us, our comfortable environment has been disrupted, and we must adapt to survive. And although we may have lost our jobs, our homes, or our retirements, *we have gained a freedom which allows us to further God's kingdom.*

Philip's list of accomplishments while on his missionary expedition is significant: He preached Christ to multitudes in the city of Samaria. He did miracles to prove that Jesus was the long-awaited Messiah, and these miracles were witnessed by many and spread by word-of-mouth throughout the city. He baptized the believers there. He cast-out demons. He miraculously healed the sick and paralyzed. He even converted a powerful sorcerer to the true faith of Jesus Christ. And through it all, there was great joy in that city. What a resume!

However, in order for the Samaritans to experience this great joy, there was a price to pay. And that price was: *Philip had to be persecuted.* Philip's comfort was the *one thing* which stood in the way of him fulfilling his life-purpose. And Philip's comfort was the *one thing* which kept the Samaritans from receiving the joy of knowing Jesus Christ. The point is, maybe your life has been disrupted to move you into a role of greater Christian service. Maybe God is asking *you* to pay the price required to open the flood-gates of joy for an unknown multitude of spiritually-starved people.

Before this financial upheaval, you were probably doing just fine in your own environment. You had stable employment, and you financially supported your local church. You might have even actively served there in some capacity, or participated in a short-term mission trip. Or possibly you were climbing spiritual heights by gaining the tremendous victory of personal holiness.

Certainly you have many spiritual successes and victories in your recent past, so why would God allow your faithful Christian service to be interrupted by this economic crisis? Maybe He did it for the same reason as Philip: *to use you in a greater measure.* In fact, your economic collapse might have more to do with your *past successes* in the kingdom of God than anything else. You have been a small fish in a small pond, and God is now stretching you to become a bigger fish in a bigger pond. God appreciates your track-record of spiritual success, and He is trying to spread your terrific progress across more area than ever before. Just like with Philip, *what you have to offer is too good to keep hidden any longer!*

Philip took advantage of the Jerusalem persecution, and used it as a tool to spread the message of Christ far and wide. Ever since then, God has continued to work towards world-wide evangelism. He hasn't changed His mind, or reevaluated His goals. God is still after expansion, and He wants you and me to make it happen!

You, like much of the American church, have been growing in spiritual depth to this point. Nevertheless, now is the time to transition from depth-growth to expansion-growth. It is time to make a much-needed worldwide evangelistic thrust, and there is no reason to let a perfectly good crisis-opportunity to go to waste! Instead, use it to advance the kingdom of God. Use trials to your advantage by trying something new, just like Philip did. Now that you have the time, take the mission trip you've always wanted to take. Start the ministry which has been weighing on your mind. Write the book you have always wanted to write . . . I did! Treat unemployment as your invitation to go back to school and get the training which will help you climb higher heights.

Times of change are times of opportunity. What one person sees as trouble, another sees as *opportunity.* In today's economic crisis, *somebody* is going to discover how to use the situation to their advantage. And this person will make a lot of money because of it. Likewise in today's crisis, somebody is going to do great things for God simply because they were bold enough to try. *Let this be you.* Don't wait for somebody else to rubber-stamp your ideas. *Take the initiative,* just like Philip did. *You* be the "mover and shaker" who affects an entire region for Christ. *You* be the voice crying-out in the wilderness to "prepare the way of the LORD" (Matthew 3:3, NKJV). Consider the house you lost as a chain which held you back from pursuing your ultimate life-calling. Now is a new season: no house required! You see, *now* is your greatest window of opportunity . . . don't miss it!

Just like Philip, you might not have been incredibly important where you came from, but that makes no difference. You will be a God-send to those who you encounter from now on. You will do greater things than ever before, as you leverage your circumstances to expand God's kingdom in the earth. But don't expect somebody to present you with an engraved invitation to do these great works. You will have to *take the initiative* otherwise nothing will happen. The Bible does not record that Philip was invited to go evangelize the Samaritans; most likely he simply did it of his own accord. As an alternative, Philip could have sulked in his misfortune; surely some people at the Jerusalem church did just that. But not Philip. He used this disruption as an opportunity for expansion and ultimate success. As one of the many who were scattered, he recognized an opportunity when he saw one, and used that scattering to his own advantage. If you will do the same, you will go beyond making yourself better for life; you will make *the world* better for life.

If you will take the time to read the eighth chapter of the book of the Acts of the Apostles, you will quickly realize it is all about Philip. Others are mentioned, but by and large this chapter is the account of how Philip made the most of his disrupted life by focusing on the evangelistic mission. It is his *success story*, and it all began with persecution. *Let this be the story of your crisis. Your* success story is waiting to be written, but first you have to *live* it.

In the future you will look back at this moment and recognize it as the time when you took advantage of your situation and thereby found your calling. Make the most of your difficult situation; *find a way to use it for the glory of God.* There *is* a way, and if you will seek it, you will find it. And when you have found it, then you will have found your opportunity. There are multitudes waiting for your caring touch. *Go to them.* There is an entire world waiting to hear what you have to say. *Go tell them.* Now is the time to do all you can to expand the kingdom of God. You have so much to offer, *don't hold back now.* Give it all you've got; you'll never regret it. Others will thank you, God will reward you, and you will be *better* for it.

Discussion Questions

1. Is it true that "comfort is the enemy of progress"? Explain.

2. Explain how the Jerusalem church had *settled*.

3. Has this chapter helped you discover areas in which you have also settled for less than living up to your potential? Explain.

4. What is God's goal? Has it changed since 2000 years ago? Why or why not?

5. Explain the two different types of growth, and describe the purpose of each.

6. How did God "help" the Jerusalem church to accomplish *expansion-growth*?

7. How does God sometimes "help" comfortable Christians to "expand" (i.e., to get involved in His mission to evangelize the entire world)?

8. Have you been inspired by learning about Philip? What truths have you learned from this biblical character?

9. Explain how "times of change are times of opportunity." What does it require to make this a reality *for you*?

10. Has this chapter given you a new way to look at your difficulties? Explain.

11. Will you commit to being an *expansion-minded* Christian? If so, in what practical ways can you leverage your situation to help expand the kingdom of God?

14

Be Willing

How to Turn Your Financial Hardship into Your Finest Hour

(1 PETER 5:10–11)

I do the very best I know how, the very best I can, and I mean to keep on doing so until the end.

—ABRAHAM LINCOLN

TWELVE YEARS AGO I stepped aboard a U.S. Coast Guard ship (otherwise known as a "Cutter") as a new engineering officer (in-training). During my two years aboard the Cutter *Tahoma*, I quickly learned what the Coast Guard was all about—saving lives. We performed drug interdiction on the high seas and enforced safety standards for the maritime industry, but our drop-everything-and-go mission was search and rescue. The report of a monstrous storm would send most ships in to port . . . but not ours. Even in those conditions, if a distress call was made, we would head into the storm as fast as our two engines would propel us. We went where nobody else would go in order to help someone in danger. This is a noble calling, and a dangerous one.

On my cutter, we didn't get "the call" often, but when there was a vessel in distress, life onboard *Tahoma* changed. The General Alarm bell sounded, and the constant training stopped. Extra lookouts scanned the horizon with binoculars, searching for hints of life. The vessel's pitching and rolling increased in magnitudes as we pushed our way into the fury of the tempest which held other ships in its death-grip. And the engines were pushed to maximum operating speed while watch-standers closely monitored every gage. *The call* must be answered, and we *needed* those engines in order to save lives.

However, there were more changes than that. The *people* changed, too. Bickering stopped. Personal problems were set-aside. And team-work began—*real* teamwork. We had to all work together to succeed in our mission, and everybody knew it. The interesting thing is, although we all understood that *the call* would put our lives in danger, we didn't care. Anticipation permeated the atmosphere, and we knew this was the culmination of all of our training. This was what we signed-up for. This was our *finest hour.*

You might think our finest hour happened only once, but in reality, it happened each time we got *the call*. In other words, it was never very far away. Likewise, *your* "finest hour" is not so far away, either. In fact, you can make it happen *today*, if you just have the right ingredients. These ingredients are neither complicated nor elusive. They are actually commonplace for the Christian. The three key ingredients include: one plump and ripe *opportunity*, one heavy dose of *ability*, and just a dash of *willingness*. If you combine these three elements, then you are *guaranteed* to produce your *finest hour* . . . every time. But if any one of these three is missing, then at best nothing happens, or at worst disaster happens.

If you are in a tempest of your own, then *now* is your "plump and ripe *opportunity.*" Or, as we would say in the Coast Guard, now is *your call*. Moreover, the greater the disaster is, the greater the opportunity. Don't look at your trials as though you have no chance to overcome. Friend, you are *guaranteed to overcome* as long as you have the other two ingredients. Rarely do you have the option to choose your *finest hour*. Typically it chooses you, arriving in the form of an unexpected crisis. Maybe you have never had such a tremendous opportunity to succeed placed before you, but it is here now!

The second ingredient is "one heavy dose of *ability*." You probably assume that you don't have "the right stuff" to overcome your situation. You are right. You *don't* have what it takes, and *neither do I*. This is why the second ingredient of "one heavy dose of ability" is not added to the mixture by *you*, but by *God*. The outcome of your trials does not depend on *your* abilities; it depends on *God's* abilities.

You see, *none of us* have what it takes to overcome in life. Jesus knew this, which is why He said, "I am the vine, you *are* the branches. He who abides in Me, and I in him, bears much fruit; for without Me you can do nothing" (John 15:5, NKJV). The Lord Jesus promised that if you will just *keep yourself attached to Him*, then you will have *all the ability you could ever need* to overcome your situation. After experiencing this, the Apostle Paul was unashamed to tell people: "We are not saying that we can do this work ourselves. It is God who makes us able to do all that we do" (2 Corinthians 3:5, NCV). And it is God who will make you able to do all that *you* do, as well. In fact, He has already been preparing you for this.

As you face the swells of hardship and the torrents of disaster, remember this above all: *God did not set you up for failure.* Your circumstances may have been a surprise to you, but they were not a surprise to the Lord of heaven and earth. Before time began, He knew *everything* you would face throughout your life—even this. The Lord saw this storm building on your horizon long before you were born, and He intentionally trained you to handle it. You may not *feel* ready, but you *are* ready. Without ever being pushed to your limits, you would never know how great you can be! The lessons you learned in church will now give you lessons to draw-on to endure this storm. Your daily Bible reading will give you encouragement and direction. You will gain hope from the time you invest in praising the Lord. And your prayer-time will now become your lifeline to sanity. You have the right tools and the right training to overcome, however, these things will be of no value in your trials *if you don't use them.*

This brings us to the third and final ingredient of "just a dash of *willingness.*" The *opportunity* is present, in the form of a significant life-problem. You have the necessary *ability*, in that the Lord will make you more-than-able to overcome any situation. So, the only thing you can bring to the table is *your willingness.* God won't force you to do things His way. You must decide to be willing to do things His way. In other words, *the outcome of your crisis only depends on your willingness.* If you are willing, God will add some of His "super" to your "natural," and when this happens, you are guaranteed to overcome! You don't have to be *strong*—God will be strong for you. You don't have to be *smart*—God will be smart for you. The only thing you have to be is *willing.* If you are willing, then your trails are sure to produce positive results. And your financial hardship is guaranteed to become *your finest hour*.

In my own personal story, I was waiting for full-time employment while my family and I were on the verge of being forced to vacate our apartment and move into our three-person dome tent. We were busy packing our meager belongings into a small storage facility, in preparation for our new "tent-city" home. When friends and family members would ask about our future plans, we would tell them about our minivan and tent. Thinking we were out of our minds, they invited us to drive cross-country to stay with them until I could find a job. Since we had nowhere else to go, we accepted. It appeared this trial would turn into an exciting cross-country adventure for my family!

Then, in the midst of packing, my telephone rang. It was one of the engineering companies which I had recently applied to—they called to offer me a job! In fact, I received offers for *two* engineering positions! Although engineering was not my first post-seminary career choice, it turned-out to be my *only* choice in time of need. So I accepted one of these positions and (strangely enough) moved my family to . . . *Malta*. Not the *island* of Malta, that is, but the *town* of Malta in New York State. Also during this time, my long-time dream of becoming a Christian author was realized as Wipf and Stock Publishers accepted my first book (the one in your hands right now) for publication! God had not only ended our storm, but He also provided an added blessing through it. He replaced our nightmare with a dream-come-true! Friend, if God did it for me, then He can do it for *you*!

Through this book we explored the various biblical reasons why God may have allowed your difficulties to happen. In addition, I challenged you to stop focusing on regaining your lost comforts, and instead, to use your circumstances to make yourself *better for life*. Then I provided you with practical tools to help you accomplish this. Furthermore, it was discussed that these practices were not designed to change your circumstances, but were intended to change *you* while in your circumstances. At this point I want to encourage you to tell *your* story on this book's website, www.BetterForLifeBook.com. Sharing the lessons you have learned from life and this book will not only reinforce truths you have learned, but it will also encourage and inspire others who are in their own mess and need to hear of your experience. But the story is not over—there is more.

The third and final premise of this book is this: *if you will work to fix yourself, then God will work to fix your situation.* I have intentionally reserved this nugget of truth for the end of this book, because it can easily distract your attention away from the goal of spiritual progress, and thereby spoil your motivation to overcome. However, by now you understand that God's goals for us while in our trials are not typically our own goals. Remember, *God is not so concerned with making life better for us; He is interested in making us better for life.* It takes a major mind-shift in order to see things God's way, and to get onboard with His plan of improving our spiritual lives. Part of this is eliminating spiritual laziness from our personal agenda, and enlisting our *active participation* in our own spiritual growth. These have been the two major goals of this book thus far.

With this in mind, now is the time to let you in on a little secret. If you have taken-to-heart this book's message of *bettering yourself through your storm*, then I can say with confidence that I believe your storm will soon end. Storms always end. Storms *must* end. Mine did, and so will yours. Further, in most cases, the end-date of your storm will be based on your willingness to use it as God intended: to improve your spiritual life. You see, although God does not often *initiate* a person's trials, He always *oversees* them. While a person is complaining, God's hands are tied. However, when the individual *stops* complaining, choosing rather to apply their efforts to becoming a more devoted follower of Christ *through their trials*, exciting things start happening. They learn this priceless lesson, their life is indeed transformed, and God's compassion is aroused. And when all these things happen, the trial's end is typically near. If you have been striving to embrace the principles of this book, and have been observing the "how to" practices contained in it, then you are not only becoming a better *you* for it, but you will also soon watch your personal storm fade away in the distance. Just when you have come to terms with your predicament and pain, they will both disappear.

This process brings to mind the principle of childbirth. In the birthing process, laboring is difficult and extremely painful for the woman. So is life when you are laboring to birth a new chapter in your life-story. The night before Jesus was crucified He prepared His disciples for their transition using the same analogy. "A woman, when she is in labor, has sorrow because *her hour has come*; but as soon as she has given birth to the child, she no longer remembers the anguish, for joy that a human being has been born into the world" (John 16:21, NKJV, emphasis added). Clearly, your current transition is different than the one the disciples faced 2000 years ago, nonetheless it is still a transition into a new phase of life. Your own personal *hour has come*. When the new chapter of your life-story is finally "born," you will quickly forget the pain it took to get you there.

One of my favorite Bible verses is: "Those who plant in tears will harvest with shouts of joy. They weep as they go to plant their seed, but they sing as they return with the harvest" (Psalms 126:5–6, NLT). If you could measure the depth of your pain and the amount of your tears shed as a result of your trials and tribulations, it would probably be quite significant. Mine was. The good news, however, is that this same measure will be the amount of fullness and rejoicing you will experience when it is all over. And *that* is worth shouting about!

For most readers of this book who have made a determined effort to practice its principles, it is only a matter of time before things change. When your situation improves, God will wipe away every tear from your eyes (see Revelation 21:4). You will forget the pain and the suffering, and you will enjoy the great blessings of your reward. Or, as James puts it, "Blessed *is* the man who endures temptation; for when he has been approved, he will receive *the crown of life* which the Lord has promised to those who love Him" (James 1:12, NKJV, emphasis added). Your tears and heartaches will be a faint memory, as you are filled with the blessings and goodness of God.

When your problems are resolved, however, don't assume your challenges are over. They are not. In fact, your next challenge can be just as difficult. It is to *remember the lessons you have learned*. When life becomes joyful once again, it is easy to forget the truths which you discovered while in your struggles, and the practices which you began there. This is dangerous, because you can quickly backslide from the progress you made in becoming *a better you*.

For example, finally settled into your new life, it would be easy to forget to help others. You might decide that thanking God for the small stuff is no longer necessary. Or striving to change your world for Christ may lose its importance, in light of the comfort you have reestablished. In short, as humans we are prone to fall back into bad habits of spiritually laziness. Yet this would be a tragic departure from the better person you have worked hard to become. Remember, this book is about making you better *for life*, not just better for a brief moment.

My prescription for this stage of life is to continue the practices which you have begun with this book. When you are back on your feet, budget a small portion of your income to give to less-fortunate families. You can *always* find someone who could use a little help, and it is in your best-interest to help them. Continue to scan the fields of your heart for *stones* which need to be uprooted to ensure your relationship with Christ thrives. Although these stones are often only uncovered during our trials and tribulations, they are grown during seasons of comfort; find them and remove them early. Praise God for the big blessings, *and* thank Him for the small stuff. He is worthy of our thanks in *all seasons* and for *all things.* And keep your heart and your actions engaged in God's world-wide evangelistic mission. If each of us will make an effort to do just a little, we can collectively get a whole lot done. It might even be a good idea to quickly re-read this book when life gets better.

The truth is, these things are not only to be done when we are in difficulties; they are to be practiced continually by every Christian. Until the day when God chooses to step-in and improve your lot, your job is to become better for life. Moreover, after that, your job will *still be* to become better for life. As an added measure of motivation, the Bible explains that each believer's reward in heaven will be based upon their level of diligence in the Lord's work. "Therefore, my beloved brethren, be steadfast, immovable, always abounding in the work of the Lord, knowing that your labor is not in vain in the Lord" (1 Corinthians 15:58, NKJV).

You are guaranteed a reward for every ounce of effort you put into your Christian walk, so make the most of your trials while you still have the chance! There is no better time to improve yourself than when your situation goes to somewhere-in-a-hand-basket. You have the *opportunity*, and God will give you the *ability*. All that is needed at this point is your *willingness.* Your time of financial hardship is only *one decision away* from becoming *your finest hour.* Make the right decision, and get onboard with God's plan-A for you. In the years to come you will thank God for this time of trials, remembering that through it you became *better for life!*

> But may the God of all grace, who called us to His eternal glory by Christ Jesus, after you have suffered a while, perfect, establish, strengthen, and settle *you.* To Him *be* the glory and the dominion forever and ever. Amen (1 Peter 5:10–11, NKJV).

Discussion Questions

1. What are the three key ingredients to one's "finest hour"? Explain why each is necessary.

2. Do you get to choose your *finest hour*? How often is it possible to have *your finest hour*? Why?

3. Explain where the three "key ingredients" come from. Which element must come from us?

4. Has your time of difficulty caught God by surprise? Do you believe that God has prepared you for this time? Why or why not?

5. Has the author's personal story encouraged you? How so, or why not?

6. What is the third (and final) premise to this book? Do you believe it to be true? Why or why not?

7. What has been the goal of this book up to this chapter?

8. Have you taken to-heart the message of this book? Have you been trying to apply the principles of this book?

9. Do you believe that God has been working behind the scenes to resolve your situation?

10. Can you imagine what your life will look like, when God steps-in to restore your situation? Does the thought of this give you hope?

11. When life does get better, what will be your next challenge? How will you handle it? Why is it so important to handle this challenge the right way?

12. What *one lesson* or *one thought* from this book will you remember in the years to come? Explain why.

13. What life-story or faith-building lesson could you use to encourage others on this book's website? Would you consider sharing it on this website, as a way to inspire others?

Notes

Chapter 1

1. "Special Report: The World's Billionaires", ed. Luisa Kroll, Matthew Miller and Tatiana Serafin, *Forbes,* 03.11.09, 06:00PM EDT, http://www.forbes.com/2009/03/11/worlds-richest-people-billionarires-2009-billionaires_land.html.

Chapter 2

1. Tad Friend, "Letter from California: Jumpers (The fatal grandeur of the Golden Gate Bridge)," interview with Ken Baldwin, *New Yorker,* October 13, 2003, http://www.newyorker.com/archive/2003/10/13/031013fa_fact.

Chapter 5

1. "Man Dies After Paramedic Refuses to Enter Dirty Home," *Fox News,* Feb 27, 2009, http://www.foxnews.com/story/0,2933,501766,00.html (accessed March 28, 2010).

Chapter 7

1. Geinrich Fredrich Wilhelm Gesenius, *Gesenius's Hebrew and Chaldee Lexicon to the Old Testament Scriptures,* trans. Samuel Prideaux Tregelles (London: Samuel Bagster and Sons, Paternoster Row, 1857). Blue Letter Bible. "Dictionary and Word Search for Qayin (Strong's 7014)". Blue Letter Bible. 1996–2010. 28 Mar 2010. <http://www.blueletterbible.org/lang/lexicon/Lexicon.cfm?strongs=H7014>

2. Geinrich Fredrich Wilhelm Gesenius, *Gesenius's Hebrew and Chaldee Lexicon to the Old Testament Scriptures,* trans. Samuel Prideaux Tregelles (London: Samuel Bagster and Sons, Paternoster

Row, 1857). Blue Letter Bible. "Dictionary and Word Search for Hebel (Strong's 1893)." Blue Letter Bible. 1996–2010. 28 Mar 2010. <http://www.blueletterbible.org/lang/lexicon/Lexicon.cfm?strongs =H1893>

Chapter 9

1. Carl Ludwig Wilibald Grimm, *A Greek-English Lexicon of the New Testament being Grimm's Wilke's Clavis Novi Testamenti*, trans., rev., and enl. by Joseph Henry Thayer (New York: American Book Co., 1889). Blue Letter Bible. "Dictionary and Word Search for skandalizō (Strong's 4624)." Blue Letter Bible. 1996–2010. 28 Mar 2010. <http://www.blueletterbible.org/lang/lexicon/Lexicon. cfm?strongs=G4624>